LET'S REASON TOGETHER

...Youths' A-Z

LET's REASON TOGETHER
...Youths' A-Z
BOOK 1

© Oluwakemi. O. Ola - Ojo 2010

Let's Reason Together
...Youths' A-Z

Published by Protokos Publishers, United Kingdom
© 2010 by Oluwakemi Ola-Ojo

ISBN – 978-0-9557898-7-8

ALL RIGHTS RESERVED
No part of this publication may be reproduced, stored in a retrieval system, or transmitted in any form or by any means without prior permission of the Publishers.

Protokos Publishers 2010
P.O. Box 48424
SE15 2YL, London, United Kingdom.

DEDICATION

This book is dedicated to Youths and Young People all over the world.

'Let's Reason Together ...Youths' A-Z

*1. **Remember now thy Creator in the days of thy youth, while the evil days come not**, nor the years draw nigh, when thou shalt say, I have no pleasure in them;*
2. While the sun, or the light, or the moon, or the stars, be not darkened, nor the clouds return after the rain:
³ In the day when the keepers of the house shall tremble, and the strong men shall bow themselves, and the grinders cease because they are few, and those that look out of the windows be darkened,
4. And the doors shall be shut in the streets, when the sound of the grinding is low, and he shall rise up at the voice of the bird, and all the daughters of music shall be brought low;
5. Also when they shall be afraid of that which is high, and fears shall be in the way, and the almond tree shall flourish, and the grasshopper shall be a burden, and desire shall fail: because man goeth to his long home, and the mourners go about the streets:
6. Or ever the silver cord be loosed, or the golden bowl be broken, or the pitcher be broken at the fountain, or the wheel broken at the cistern.

7. Then shall the dust return to the earth as it was: and the spirit shall return unto God who gave it.
8. Vanity of vanities, saith the preacher; all is vanity.
9. And moreover, because the preacher was wise, he still taught the people knowledge; yea, he gave good heed, and sought out, and set in order many proverbs.
10. The preacher sought to find out acceptable words: and that which was written was upright, even words of truth.
11. The words of the wise are as goads, and as nails fastened by the masters of assemblies, which are given from one shepherd.
12. And further, by these, my son, be admonished: of making many books there is no end; and much study is a weariness of the flesh.
13. **Let us hear the conclusion of the whole matter: Fear God, and keep his commandments: for this is the whole duty of man.**
14. **For God shall bring every work into judgment, with every secret thing, whether it be good, or whether it be evil.**

[Ecclesiastes 12: 1-14 emphasis mine.]

Acknowledgment

God is to be praised for the insight and anointing He blessed me with in writing this book.

I am grateful to God for my family and friends whose understanding and co-operation has blessed my life and writing.

I am very much honoured to have Pastor Mary McCauley write the foreword in spite of her busy schedule. Her prayers and encouragements have blessed my life.

Thanks to Mrs. Sumbo Oladipo for editing this book and for her support, encouragement and creativity.

Thanks to all who found time to read and comment on this book for their invaluable comments and encouragement.

And finally, I thank Prex Holdings for the book cover design and Protokos Publishers for the excellent work they have done and for making my dreams come true by their efforts in publishing and marketing my books.

FOREWORD

At last, a holistic approach to the needs of youth and youth workers/teachers; an informative, educational, relational, empowering, equipping and resourceful book from a Christian perspective. A life-giving and enriching resource book; good as an icebreaker, discussion-starter and Bible study especially for new believers and born again youths. This is a super manual for youth workers to use.

Oluwakemi is a seasoned prolific writer whose work and experience with children and youth over the years has led her into writing this valuable book. This is a book for youth workers, families with teenagers and youths, individual youth and youth clubs. Its lessons are applicable to believers and unbelievers and cut across every known barrier.

Pastor Mary McCauley
Co-ordinator, Open Gate
DR2 DV8
2 Union Road
Croydon
CRO 2XU

… 'Let's Reason Together …Youths' A-Z

CONTENTS *Page*

Dedication v
Acknowledgement viii
Foreword ix
Content x
Introduction xiv
Strategy for use xvi

A:	Attitude	21
B:	Bible	37
C:	Choices	47
D:	Dreams	63
E:	Endurance	73
F:	Forgiveness	83
G:	Giving	93
H:	Humility	105
I:	Integrity	113
J:	Justice	121
K:	Knowledge	133
L:	Love	145
M:	Miracles	159
N:	Networking	169
O:	Oath	179

P:	Presentation	189
Q:	Quest	199
R:	Respect	209
S:	Sin	219
T:	Truth	233
U:	Unity	247
V:	Vacation	257
W:	Wealth	265
X:	Xenophobic	275
Y:	Yoke	283
Z:	Zest	291

Summary	297
Opportunity to Become a Christian	300
Other Books	302
Useful Links	312

'Let's Reason Together …Youths' A-Z

BOOK 2

CONTENTS *Page*

Dedication
Acknowledgement
Foreword
Content
Introduction
Strategy for use

A: Anger
B: Betrayal
C: Contentment
D: Drugs
E: Examination
F: Faith
G: Growth
H: Homosexuality
I: Ignorance
J: Jealousy
K: Kindness
L: Lawful
M: Money

'Let's Reason Together ...Youths' A-Z

N: Name
O: Obedience
P: Praise
Q: Quiet time
R: Rejection
S: Sex
T: Temptations
U: Unbelief
V: Vision
W: Words
X: X-ray
Y: Youth
Z: Zeal

Summary
Opportunity to Become a Christian
Other Books
Useful Links

Introduction

Welcome to 'Let's Reason Together …Youths' A-Z, where we shall discuss issues relating to teenagers and youths' lives from Biblical and other perspectives.

In learning to read and write in **English**, children start with learning the **alphabet** from A to Z. A good knowledge of this forms the basic foundation for future education and communication. In the same way, this book focuses on the A-Z of teenage or youth life. It can be used personally or in a group study. It is advisable that you focus on **one letter of the alphabet** per week to get the best out of the study and exercises. Don't be put off if some of the letters take you more than a week to get through.

For use in a group study, one of the youths should be chosen to moderate; he or she should prepare to lead by reading the subject ahead of the study, and adding any relevant local information, as the treatment of the topics is not exhaustive. The moderator should ask the questions as outlined in this book but may add other relevant questions. There should be flexibility in the discussions and members of the group are encouraged to participate in the sessions. It is good to allow group members to act as moderator in turns with the different **letters of the alphabet.**

It is a good idea also to give a few minutes for members of the group to share testimonies on how helpful the previous lesson has been to them. The adult supervising the group should give an altar call at the end of the discussions, and adequate time ought to be spent afterwards to counsel those who need it.

Along with each topic, a key phrase and scripture are provided as a reminder of what the **letter** stands for and it is my prayer that these will be committed to memory for present and future guidance.

Finally, at the end of each topic there is an exercise section and some prayer points for the individual or the group.

STRATEGY FOR USE

Someone amongst the teenagers or youth is chosen to be the moderator; he/she should have read the information/text ahead of the discussions, be prepared for leading, and is allowed to add any relevant local information as the list has not been exhausted. He/she moderates by asking the questions as outlined in this book but may add other relevant questions. Members of the group are equally encouraged to participate/contribute to the discussion. The adult supervising the group gives an altar call at the end of the discussions, and appropriate time is spent counselling those who may so require afterwards.

It is good to allow group members to act as moderator in turns. The moderator and the supervising adult for the day should also have read the manuscript ahead of the meeting.

There is more to each topic chosen per alphabet. There is need to make the discussion as relevant to the community/people as much as it is practicable therefore there should be flexibility in the discussions.

'Let's Reason Together ...Youths' A-Z

A key phrase/scripture is given to help each teenager or youth to remember what the alphabet stands for and it is my prayers that these will be committed into memory for present and future needs/guidance.

As a good gesture, I have included some write-up on some additional alphabets with different topics on our website which is free for you. Do please tell your friends about the series and how it has helped you and we love to hear from you too. Write to us or visit www.protokospublishers.com and leave us your comments. God bless you real good.

ATTITUDE

ATTITUDE

"My attitude will determine my altitude in life".

*"Thy Word is a lamp unto my feet,
and a light unto my path"
[Psalms 119:105].*

Question For Consideration/Discussion:
1. What is an attitude?
2. Is there is a right or wrong attitude?
3. How do you know if an attitude is right or wrong?
4. What is your attitude to God?
5. What is your attitude to your parents and those in authority over you?
6. What is your attitude to yourself – studies, health, and self-esteem?
7. What is your attitude to work and the future?
8. What is your attitude to money and wealth?
9. Attitude influencers what or who are these?
10. Attitude and altitude how are they related?
11. Some positive and negative attitudes.

What is an Attitude?

An attitude could be described as the way of behaving, mind-set, approach or way of thinking, or what is really inside a person that is outwardly expressed - just to mention a few. There is in most instances a right or wrong attitude to every situation of life confronting anyone, teenagers and youths especially.

To find out if an attitude is right, ask yourself a few questions e.g. will God be pleased with what I am doing, about to do or I have done? The Bible will provide the check you need to determine whether your attitude is right or wrong in a given situation; or will my parents or whoever you hold in highest esteem be pleased to see what you are doing now?

Your attitude to God will determine your attitude to Him and all that concerns Him.

Do you belief that He exists, that He created all including you, and He is alive and well? Do you believe that He loves you just as you are and that He is able to use your past and pain to promote you? How often many think they don't need God in life! Some think by their own efforts they have achieved all that they have done but it is a known fact that without God our Creator, no life exists, let alone achieves

ATTITUDE

anything. A fool says in his/her heart that there is no God. What is your attitude to worshipping God, believing His words and obeying them, etc? Are you grateful for every blessing you have received?

What is your attitude to your parents and those in authority over you?

Is it that which shows love, respect and submission or otherwise? The Bible says you are to *"honour your father and mother that thy days may be long in the land which the Lord thy God giveth thee"* [*Exodus 20:12*] and *"Children, obey your parents in the Lord: for this is right. Honour thy father and mother; (which is the first commandment with a promise;"* [*Ephesians 6:1-2*]. Your parents and those in authority over you like your teachers, government etc, might not have as much education as yourself, but they certainly have more experience in life than you.

Pray for them that they might guide you in the right direction in life. Even when they mistakenly guide you wrongly, the Lord will turn it around and help you.

'Let's Reason Together ...Youths' A-Z

What is your attitude to yourself?

Is it love or hatred? I hate my leg, face, size etc you might say but must you look like someone else? What thoughts do you have of yourself? You are unique, beautiful and wonderfully made even as you are. God made you, beautiful and unique unto Himself. You were not an accident that happened as some parents tell their children; you were in God's thoughts and plans. He has an assignment for you that only you will be able to fulfil in this life.

'For thou hast possessed my reins: thou hast covered me in my mother's womb. I will praise thee; for I am fearfully and wonderfully made: marvellous are thy works; and that my soul knoweth right well. My substance was not hid from thee, when I was made in secret, and curiously wrought in the lowest parts of the earth. Thine eyes did see my substance, yet being unperfect; and in thy book all my members were written, which in continuance were fashioned, when as yet there was none of them. How precious also are thy thoughts unto me, O God! How great is the sum of them! If I should count them, they are more in number than the sand: when I awake, I am still with thee'. *[Psalms 139:13- 18]*

A healthy, positive attitude towards yourself will make you watch what you put in your body and how you treat or allow others around you to treat your body. Do you give

ATTITUDE

your body enough rest, good exercise and good nutritional foods? Medically we know that smoking, drinking and other such vices are poisonous and dangerous to the physical body in the same way that pornography pollutes the mind; and adultery, fornication, uncleanness, lasciviousness, idolatry, witchcraft, hatred, variance, emulations, wrath, strife, seditions, heresies, envying, murders, drunkenness and revelling, pollute the spirit and all lead to destruction sooner or later *[Galatians 5: 19-21]* Men and women who end up as prostitutes or strippers many times do so as they have no value or respect for their lives/bodies. Often, they see their bodies as an object such as shoes to be used, abused and discarded. Many have sold their bodies at some point in time in exchange for some financial gratification only to find out that from that affair – singular or multiple – they sold their future therefore, their destiny, by virtue of the outcome of their actions. Others, by so doing, have contacted incurable sexually transmitted diseases (STDs), sometimes including HIV and AIDS. Remember that you have only one life to live; there are no spares, so appreciate and value God's gift to you by taking good care of your body! It is not a question of who loves you or does not; rather, you owe yourself love. After all, God demands that you love your neighbour as yourself. God has imputed in you all that you need for astonishing success in spite of all the odds against you. Proclaim to yourself, *'I (insert your name) can do all things through Christ Jesus who strengthens me'* *[Philippians 4:13]*.

What is your attitude to your studies or the trade you are learning?

Average refers to the common, the regular. As an average student, you do just enough to stay above board, or as they say, to keep your head above water, but if you must lead, if you must stand shoulders above your peers, you must work extra hard, and go the extra mile in your studies or choice of trade. Distinction comes with diligence and it is only the diligent that stand before kings. A good pass in the GCE / GSCE examinations provides the foundation on which your admission to a higher institution is guaranteed. So is the result of your vocational qualification the foundation for progress in your vocational field of interest. Build a solid foundation today in your education for your future will depend on it.

What is your attitude towards your health?

Health is wealth. What do you feed to your body, mind and soul? Do you live to eat or eat to live? Junk food and carbonated chemical packed drinks will do you more harm than good. Exercise is equally good for your health and should not be neglected. Plain clean water is many times better than any man-made drink or alcohol or wine. Fresh fruits and vegetables will do you more good than any candy or sweet. Watch what you read or feed your mind on for they will affect your thoughts and what flows out of you – whether rivers of living water or otherwise.

What is your Attitude towards your work and future?

What you build into yourself as a teenager or youth may help or hinder your future. If you are the lazy type, to get or keep a job might be difficult in years to come but if you are the dedicated hardworking type, you possibly are on your way to standing before Kings *[Proverbs 22:29].* Joseph and Daniel were hardworking and diligent in all their duties, no wonder they became successful in their callings and were able to affect their generations *[Daniel 1:3-20, 2:48-49. Genesis 39:1-21, 41: 38-57].* If you decide to sleep when your mates are working, you will work when they are sleeping.

What is your Attitude towards Money and Wealth?

What will you do to get money or wealth? Money in itself is not bad but the love of money is the root of all evil *[Hebrews*

13:5b]. Have you soiled your name, life for some wealth or money that has wings and could fly away as a bird? *[Proverbs 23:5]*. What are you prepared to do to get money? Wealth without the fear of God is the fear of everything and no peace.

What will you do when you become wealthy? Wealth that is not shared with your family, the poor and ministry work is 'money miss road' as they say in some culture. It is good to know that only the blessings of the Lord makes rich and adds no sorrow to it *[Proverbs 10:22]*.

Attitude Influencers:
These are things or people who by your interaction with them influence your attitude positively or negatively.

GOOD	**BAD**
God	*Satan*
Church	*World*
Good Peers	*Bad Peers*
Good Christian Clubs	*Night Clubs, Casinos, Bars*
Christian Music, Bible Study	*Drugs/Cigarettes/Alcohol/Wine*

An altitude is described as height, elevation and height above sea level. The key phrase implies that your manner of behaviour, mind-set, approach or way of thinking will ultimately determine how far or how high in life you will go.

ATTITUDE

Examples of Positive And Negative Attitudes

Good self-esteem	Poor self-esteem
Laughter	Self-pity
Giving	Self-centredness
Humility	Pride
Forgiveness	Un-forgiveness
Praise and worship to God	Murmuring, Grumbling, Anger
Godly love	Lust
Speaking the truth	Lying
Hard work	Laziness

Attitude to Self

Permit me to share this story I once heard. A woman was having severe medical problems with her legs for some time (not a short time though). The Doctors could not do much to help her. She was in excruciating pains and agony and she called for prayers.

During intercession, the Lord revealed that for many years, she had always confessed that she hated her legs and you guess, that was the loophole the enemy needed to attack and afflict her health, family, life, finance etc. Her confession and attitude towards her legs was the cause of her trouble. She confessed her sins to God, asked for His forgiveness and God healed her.

What is your attitude to yourself and all that pertains to you? *"As he thinketh in his heart, so is he"* *[Proverbs 23:7a]*.

Here are some healthy tips to help your attitude.

12 Healthy Attitudes towards myself

1. I Know God created me and that He loves me *(Jeremiah 31:3)*
2. I have shortcomings and I want to change. I believe that God is working in my life each day; while He is, I can still accept and enjoy myself.
3. Everyone has faults; I am not a failure because I am not perfect.
4. I am working with God to overcome my faults, but there will always be something to work on; therefore I will not be discouraged when He convicts me of an attitude that I need to work on.
5. I want people to like me but my sense of worth is not dependent on them. Jesus has already demonstrated my worth by dying for me.
6. I will not be controlled by what others say, think or do. If they reject me I will survive, for God has promised never

ATTITUDE

to reject me as long as I keep on believing.

7. No matter how often I fail I will not give up, because God is with me, He has promised to strengthen and to sustain me as long as I live *(Hebrews 13:5)*.
8. I like myself, I do not like everything I do, and I want to change - but I refuse to put myself down.
9. I am acceptable to God through the blood of Jesus *(Ephesians 2:8-9)*.
10. God has a plan for my life and I am going to fulfil it; I have God-given gifts and I intend to use them to glorify Him.
11. In myself, I am nothing, but in Christ I am everything I need to be.
12. I can do whatever God calls me to do, through the powers of Him who dwells in me *(Philippians 4:13). Amen.*

© Bob Gass WORD FOR TODAY 2000.

EXERCISE

- Identify at least five good attitudes that you have.
- Identify not more than three bad attitudes that you have.
- Evaluate how you can enhance your good attitudes.
- Evaluate how you can reduce your bad attitudes.
- Identify one Godly person of your gender that can be your mentor and monitor your progress as you work on your positive and negative attitudes and contact that person today.

PRAYER POINTS

Dear God, please help me to have Godly attitudes in Jesus' name.

God please help me to have good attitudes towards myself.

May my attitude to the authorities over me honour You always.

ATTITUDE

'Let's Reason Together ...Youths' A-Z

MY PERSONAL NOTES

BIBLE

"The Bible is my atlas for a successful life".
"God's words are pure, sure and true".

"This book of the law shall not depart out of my mouth; but I shall meditate therein day and night, that I may observe to do according to all that is written therein: for then God shall make my way prosperous, and then I shall have good success." [Joshua 1:8; emphasis mine]

Questions For Consideration/Discussion:
1. What is the Bible?
2. Who wrote the Bible?
3. Who was the Bible written for?
4. Can the Bible be trusted?
5. The Bible and the other books.
6. Do you believe in the Bible? Why or why not?
7. Is the Bible still relevant to us today?
8. How to benefit best from the Bible.

What is the Bible?

It is the book that contains God's written word to mankind. It is also God's love letter to the world. It is the only book that does not need any update as it is full and rich and its contents knows no boundary of generation, technology or knowledge (the word generation already covers millennium – both speak of time). It has outlived every king, kingdom, technology, or science. To every generation, the Bible is as relevant as when it was first written. Over the years, it has been translated into several languages and dialects. Since some languages are changing themselves, the Bible has been translated in line and to accommodate the changes in these languages e.g. English – we have the original Kings James version that was full of *"thou shalt", "maketh"*, etc. and other English versions such as the New International Version (NIV), New King James Version, Living Bible version, American Version, Revised Standard Version (RSV) and New Revised Standard Version etc. The context of all these is the same but each has been written in a way that accommodates the various English expressions.

Who wrote the Bible?

Unlike any other book, it was inspired by God through the Holy Spirit that enabled many people (forty people) over many hundreds of years *(about a thousand years or more)* to write and compile.

It has two main sections, the Old Testament and the New Testament. It contains sixty-six books, thirty-nine in the Old Testament and twenty-seven in the New Testament.

Who was the Bible written for?

It was written for all mankind, irrespective of race, religion or colour, who will believe in God and it is to make people wise unto salvation through faith, which is in Christ Jesus. All scripture is given by inspiration of God, and is profitable for doctrine, for reproof, for correction, for instruction in righteousness: That the man of God may be perfect, thoroughly furnished unto all good works *[2 Timothy 3:15-17]*.

Can the bible be trusted?

This is another way of saying *"Can God be trusted?"* It is God's word/love letter to mankind. It contains no contradictions but scriptures that complement each other. There are many discoveries, excavations etc. that confirm the authenticity of the Bible above man-made theories.

The Bible and other books:

Unlike any other book written or yet to be written, only the Bible contains detailed historical background of man. Genesis, the first book of the Bible records various events such as the creation of the universe *[Genesis 1 & 2]*, the fall of man *[Genesis 3]*, the first marriage/family [Genesis 2], the flood, *[Genesis 6-9]*. The books of Joshua to Malachi records the reign of various kings, their achievements and failures, and the exploits of the prophets, and the New Testament *(Matthew to Revelation)* records the plan of God for man's redemption from sin and death and details the events of the end of the world. It is the only book that covers the agenda of God for man and indeed the whole of creation from the beginning to the end!

The Bible does not only talk about the beginning of life existence but it also contains God's law for our protection and provision, the solution to every problem man would ever face and unlike other books, the Bible tells it as it is, whether good or bad, whether it produced success or failure.

The Bible is the only book that gives adequate, proven history of the beginning of mankind on earth and also bears records of the future of humanity, some of which have begun to come to limelight in present times.

The Bible is also the only book that captures every vocation and technology, discovered or yet to be discovered, and laws that if completely obeyed, will empower mankind to be at peace with himself and with others. The Bible also offers divine information on effective infection control policy and healthy living suggestions. The Bible is an encyclopaedia on all subjects of life!

Do you believe in the Bible? why or why not?

Congratulations if you believe in the Bible and if you don't, "Why not? Make a decision to read the Bible, asking God, who inspired people to write the scriptures to reveal the truth to you and to instruct you on what to do with the word. It is the only book in which man can find total, complete transformation, wisdom for every situation, direction for every path, healing from every disease, peace with oneself and others, relationship with a living, loving God and above all peace in the storms of life.

Is the Bible still relevant to us today?

The Bible is as relevant today as it was when it was written. Life is like a journey that each person begins at birth and ends at eternity, which for some is heaven and for others ends in hell, depending on our choice. The Bible is the only atlas or map that when followed leads the follower to heaven not hell, warns the user of dangers and how to avoid them, directs the user over the mountains, hills, valleys, straight and crooked roads but at the end gets the user to the desired destination which for most people is heaven. The world in which we live in today is governed by many laws e.g. the law of gravity, the laws of sowing and reaping etc. The Bible contains the laws, which successfully governs the world *[Joshua 1:1-16, Psalms 119:1-2, 9,27, 34, 43-50,89, 92-93, 97-107,125]*.

How to get the best benefit from the Bible:

Read it and meditate on it every day, confess who the Bible says you are, observing and doing according to all that is written in it, then God will make your way prosperous and you shall have good success *[Joshua 1:8]*.

BIBLE

EXERCISE

❖ Do you have a copy of the Bible in the language that you can read and understand?
❖ How often do you get to read the Bible?
❖ Do you have a notebook where you jot down important information you receive from the Bible?
❖ Give one or two examples of where and when you found the Bible relevant to your situation.
❖ How easy it is to obey the Bible and share our findings with our friends and family?

** *To get a copy of a free Bible if you do not have one, you may contact:*
Bible Society http://www.biblica.com/ministry
Gideons - http://www.gideons.org

PRAYERS POINTS:

Lord, help me to read, meditate and understand Your word.

Lord, give me an obedient spirit to honour and obey Your words.

May God's words be made manifest in my life.

'Let's Reason Together ...Youths' A-Z

MY PERSONAL NOTES

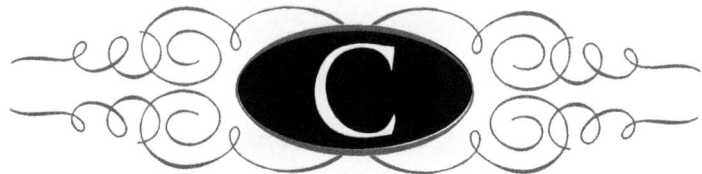

CHOICES

"My choice will either make me or break me".

"And if it seem evil unto you to serve the Lord, choose you this day whom ye will serve; whether the Gods which your fathers served that were on the other side of the flood, or the Gods of the Amorites, in whose land ye dwell: but as for me and my house, we will serve the Lord." [Joshua 24:15].

Questions for Consideration/ Discussion:
1. What is a choice?
2. Why the need for choice?
3. When do we make choice?
4. Where do I make my choice?
5. How do I make my choice?
6. Choice influencers.
7. Can my choice affect me and how?
8. What factors should I consider in making my choice?
9. The most important choice in life.
10. Result of my choice.
11. Examples of some people who made choices in the Bible.

What is Choice?

A choice could mean picking from abundance or from a variety. This could mean preference of something over or above another of the same or different thing/person or option. It could mean carefully selected preference. It could also mean an alternative to something or someone. A choice is always an expressed decision or a decision expressed.

Why the need for Choice?

God does not and will not force His will on us, but actually gives us a choice between two alternatives in every situation; between life and death, obedience and disobedience, Christ and Belial etc. This is different from the day-to-day choices we make on mundane issues like the food to eat, dress to wear etc. where we may have a variety of options to pick from. *Genesis 2:15-17.*

When do we nake Choice?

We make a choice every moment of life e.g. waking up and getting out of bed were choices that we made today. We chose to come to this meeting today and at this particular time. We choose (I hope you are all aware) what to eat or drink. For some choices, we think through before we decide and act e.g. which University, which course of study to pursue, who to marry, while for other choices we make, we act without thinking, e.g. brushing your teeth and using your colour coded toothbrush.

Where do I make my Choice?

You can make your decision anywhere, any day or at any time. It doesn't really matter where you make a decision, what is more important is the quality and content of the decision you have made.

How do I make my Choice?

Choices are made either with or without words i.e. verbally or non-verbally. Choices could be expressive (revealed) or covert (secret). Choices are often made based on information on the subject that is available to the person making the choice. This information can come from other people's experience, friends, media, books relating to the matter, family wish, likes or dislike, future aspiration, eternity, etc.

For instance, it is not unusual to have certain professions running in some families, which more or less informs the decision of children from such families to pursue such professions. This is common with a family of lawyers, architects, nurses, teachers, doctors, engineers, accountants etc.

Choice Influencers:

These are things or people who by your interaction with them influence your choice positively or negatively.

GOOD	BAD
Church	Bad clubs
Good peers	Bad peers
Good Christian Clubs	Drugs/cigarette/alcohol/wine
Bible	Occult/pornographic books

Others are:

Media (could be good or bad)
Parents/relatives and other siblings (could be good or bad)
Proposed outcome from your chosen decision

Can my Choice affect me and how?

The answer is a resounding yes. Every time you make a choice between two or more alternatives, you predetermine the outcome of your choice – whether positive or negative. For example, a person who chooses to sleep round the clock has made a decision to be poor. On the other hand, the person who chooses to work long hours has made up his/her mind to stand before kings *[Proverbs 22:29; Daniel 1:3-15]*.

A student who makes a habit of not doing his school assignment or fails to attend lectures regularly has by his/her choice decided to settle for failure or an ordinary pass position.

A youth who indulges in premarital sex has chosen to either be pregnant or make someone else pregnant, thereby becoming a premature parent as we saw in the recent case of the 12-year old boy in Britain who claimed to have fathered a child through a 15-year old girl! Such acts can make you feel used, abused and abandoned and could make you susceptible to STDs (sexually or spiritually transmitted disease). This can terminate /truncate your youth experience and forcefully get you into adult roles earlier than you are prepared for.

What factors should I consider in making my Choice?

The choices you make often have an effect on your relationships, whether vertical (God) or horizontal (Yourself, Family, Friends, Neighbours, Church, Nation). These are the people you consider when making choices in life.

The most important Choice in life

There are many important choices to make in life such as the career to pursue, who to marry, where to live, where to work but the most important choice is contingent on your very existence. *"Where will you spend eternity?"* Our existence began before we were born and life is just a journey. If Christ's return is delayed, every one born of a woman will one day keep an appointment with death! Not everyone will live long enough to have a career, get married, or get a job, and as good and important as these choices are, they are not as important as your choice in deciding where you will spend eternity. Accepting or refusing Jesus Christ as your Saviour and Redeemer is the most important choice anyone can make because that is the decision that will determine our relationship here on earth with God and our eternity when we are no more *[John 3:16-18]*.

Result of my choice

Your choice will either make you or break you. Your choice today will not only affect you but may also affect your offspring including generations yet unborn. Therefore you need to be very careful about all your decisions/choices.

CHOICES

Examples of some people who made choices in the Bible and the result of their choice(s):

TEXT	PERSON(S)	CHOICE	RESULT
Genesis 3: 1-19	**Adam and Eve**	Ate the forbidden fruit	• Both were banished from the presence of God, and driven out of the Garden. man will now till the ground and eat from the sweat of his labour; women to have labour pains. • Women to desire their husbands. • Husbands to rule over their wives. • Enmity between serpent and mankind. • Physical death.
Genesis 4:1-4	**Abel**	Gave God the right sacrifice	• Offering accepted by God.
Genesis 4:1-16	**Cain**	• Gave God the wrong sacrifice • Had a wrong attitude • Murdered Abel	• Offering rejected by God. • Was warned by God • God gave him capital punishment

Genesis 4:1-16 Genesis 6-8	**Noah**	• Obeyed God in building the ark	• Lived through the experience of the flood but his life, and those of his family members were preserved as well as the lives of the animals that were put into the ark. • God made a covenant with him, the rainbow being the sign of that covenant.

CHOICES

Reference	Person	Choices	Consequences
Gen. 12:1-9 Gen. 22:1-19	**Abram**	• Obeyed God in leaving his country • He obeyed God in sacrificing Isaac	• God made a great nation out of him. • God made his name great. • God blessed him • He became a blessing to the world. • His enemies were cursed by God. • His friends were blessed by God. • God blessed and multiplied him and his seed are to possess the gates of their enemies. • The world to be named and blessed through his seed.
Judges 13-15	**Samson**	• Disobeyed his parents in the choices of marriage partners. • Disobeyed God by eating from a dead lion	• Lost his hair, strength and anointing in the laps of Delilah. • Was bound. • Had his eyes gorged out by his enemies. • Imprisoned and grinded mill. • Ridiculed and made to entertain his enemies. • Died with the enemy.

Ruth 1-2	**Ruth**	• Went with mother in law to Bethlehem. • Accepted Jehovah God as her God. • Ministered to the physical needs of her mother in-law.	• Accepted by the people in Bethlehem • Found God and people's favour including that of Boaz. • Had her feeding needs met. • Became the wife of Boaz the millionaire. • Gave birth to Obed the grandfather of King David [Ruth 4:1-17].

CHOICES

Daniel 1:1-20 Daniel 6:1-28	**Daniel**	• Purposed not to defile himself with the King's food. • Chose to worship only Jehovah.	• Found favour with God and man. • Came first in the examinations at the end of study. • Was ten times wiser than all magicians and astrologers. • Worked in the presence of the king. • Had the gift of understanding and interpreting dreams. • Got thrown into the lion's den. • God sealed the lions' mouth so he came out without a scratch. • His enemies were thrown into the lions' den and got killed and eaten by the lions. • Decree established in favour of Jehovah. • Prospered in the land.
2 Kings 5:1-19	**Naaman**	• Obeyed Prophet Elisha and dipped in River Jordan seven times	• Got his leprosy healed. • Accepted the superiority of Jehovah.

2 Kings 5:20-22	**Gehazi**	• Lied to Naaman and took goods. • Took Naaman's goods. • Lied to Prophet Elisha.	• Cursed by Prophet Elisha – left with Naaman's leprosy. • Couldn't inherit Prophet Elisha's anointing..
John 3: 1-21	**Nichode-mus**	• Sought for Jesus Christ in the night.	• Jesus explained salvation to him. • Got saved/born again that night.

CHOICES

EXERCISE

◈ Identify some choices you have made today and how it has affected you today.
◈ Identify some choices you have made before and the outcome of such on you and your family.
◈ As a person what are the key factors that determines your choice in any situation?
◈ How has other people's choices e.g. parents affected your life thus far?
◈ What do you need to do to correct some of your previous bad choices today?

PRAYER POINTS

Teach me Lord and help me to make the right choices in life.

Forgive me Lord for the wrong decisions I have made till date.

Difficult as it may be, help me Lord in my daily decisions.

'Let's Reason Together ...Youths' A-Z

MY PERSONAL NOTES

DREAMS

DREAMS

"My future is concealed in my dreams therefore I will dream big".
"God's revelation needs no second opinion"
"Godly dreams hardly die unfulfilled".

"Where there is no vision (dream), the people perish but he that keepeth the law, happy is he." *[Proverbs 29:18]*.

Question for Consideration/ Discussion:
1. What is it?
2. What does it mean to dream?
3. Who gives dreams?
4. How to discern the source of my dream.
5. What to do with my dream.
6. What does it mean to dream?
7. Do my dreams have any relationship with my destiny?
8. How soon will my dream come to pass?
9. Dream killers or dream extinguishers?
10. Examples of dreamers.

What is it?

It may be a vision, trance, aspiration, nightmare, or flight of fantasy. It may come anytime of the day especially when sleeping.

It means having a revelation about an event that has happened or yet to happen. It may also mean to fantasize about one's desires or wishes for the future.

Who gives Dreams?

God in His mercies often communicates with us in our sleep through dreams and visions, sometimes to warn us or prepare us or to show us His plans for others or us. Satan and his agents could also communicate fears or inflict afflictions, sicknesses through dreams. A person may also fantasise about his/her future – good or bad by daydreaming. To avoid negative dreams we need to fill our hearts with God's word and counteract any ungodly dreams with the Word of God and the Blood of Jesus Christ immediately.

How to discern the source of my Dream

God-given dreams are often too vast for us to comprehend;

it often focuses on the glorious future in store for us, or warns us of an impending danger. The characteristic feature of a dream from God is the peace it produces in the heart of the dreamer and also, every dream from God must be in line with His Word and Character.

Satan's dreams are always anti-Christ or anti-God; they are full of fear and give no peace or joy.

A person is often able to fantasise or daydream with regards to his/her wishes or desires. Usually, the content of this daydream is influenced by the personality of the daydreamer.

What to do with my Dream

- ❖ Document your God given dreams *[Hab.2:3]*.
- ❖ Pray and ask God for an interpretation of your dream
- ❖ Seek Godly counsel for your dream if and when the meaning of the dream is unclear. Pharaoh needed Joseph to interpret his dreams *[Genesis 40]*, King Belshazzar needed Daniel to interpret his dreams *[Daniel 5]*.
- ❖ Cancel every devil-given dream with the word of God and the blood of Jesus Christ.
- ❖ Be careful who you share your dreams with *[Genesis 37:1- 36]*.

- ❖ Protect your dream from dream killers and destiny terminators e.g. Joseph's brothers *[Genesis 37:1- 36]*
- ❖ Obey God's instruction given to you in the dream e.g Joseph and the wise men *[Genesis 37, Matthew 2]*
- ❖ Prayerfully cooperate with God to make it come to pass *[Jacob in Genesis 30:37-42]*.
- ❖ Thank God for His revelations to you in the dream.
- ❖ Do not neglect your dream as it may hold important keys to your future.

What does it mean to Dream?

It is a divine opportunity to see your future or fantasize about your desire for your future.

Are my Dreams related to my destiny?

Yes, many times they are related.

How soon will my Dream come to pass?

Just like no one can say precisely the correct length for a piece of string so it is impossible to know precisely how soon your God-given dream will come to pass. However it shall surely come for God speaks no careless words *[Habakkuk*

2:3]. Between the time of receiving the dream and its manifestation you can be sure that:

You will go through seasons that are directly opposite to what has been revealed to you.

You will face enough crises that will test your faith in God and His revelations to you.

You may come to doubt your ability to realize that dream. You will probably be misunderstood, misquoted, misjudged, doubted etc.

You will have opportunities to throw in the towel or just join the multitude to sin – Joseph and Potiphar's wife *(Genesis 39; 7-19)*.

God's dream will come to pass in His own way, time and for His own purpose – you cannot fast forward it or delay it *(Habakkuk 2:3)*.

Dream killers or Dream extinguishers?

A dream killer is anyone or anything that toys with your dreams in a negative manner and this can occur in many ways. They could try to discredit your God, they could consider your dream as a sham or something that can never be accomplished (Joseph's brothers *(Genesis 37:1-20)*, Sanballat and Tobiah in *Nehemiah 4:1-8)*. Such persons and such relationships should be avoided like a plague.

Examples of Dreamers.
1. Abraham in Genesis 15: 12- 17
2. Isaac in Genesis 26:23-25
3. Jacob in Genesis 28:10-22
4. Laban was warned in a dream the night before he caught up with his run away son-in-law. Genesis 31:22-29
5. Joseph in Genesis 37:1-20
6. Daniel in Daniel 2: 1-23
7. The wise men in Matthew 2: 1-12
8. Joseph in Matthew 2: 13-21
9. Martin Luther King – 'I have a dream'

EXERCISE

- ◆ Identify an important dream you had recently or in times past .
- ◆ Write the dream down.
- ◆ Seek for Godly counsel if you do not know the meaning of your dream.
- ◆ Share with the group or someone who is not a dream killer an occasion when your dream came through.
- ◆ Praise God for your God-given dreams.
- ◆ Prayerfully water the dream with the word of God/ prayers and praise.
- ◆ Expect God to fulfil every dream He gives to you.
- ◆ Identify some dream killers around you and prayerfully avoid them.

PRAYER POINTS

Pray about your God-given dream.

Pray against every dream killer and every dream delayer.

Pray that God will give you all that you need to fulfil God's given dream for your life.

'Let's Reason Together ...Youths' A-Z

MY PERSONAL NOTES

ENDURANCE

"All of life's experiences are meant to sharpen and shape us so we can conform to God's image and likeness".
"We shall reap in due season if we fail or faint not".

"Looking unto Jesus the author and finisher of our faith who for the joy that was set before him endured the cross, despising the shame, and is set down at the right hand of God" [Hebrews 12:2].

Question for consideration/discussion:
1. What is it?
2. What do you need to endure?
3. Why do you need to endure?
4. Time to run or endure.
5. Does endurance pays, why or why not?
6. Rewards of endurance.

What Is It?

Endurance is the staying power, stamina, survival, patience, fortitude and continued existence of a thing or person especially when there is so much threat to that thing or person's existence.

What do you need to Endure?

Sometimes we need to endure people or things in order that we might achieve our aims. Some other time, we might have to endure a disability or situation or need until our goal is accomplished. There are times when we have to endure a situation for life! This is often the case with people who have physical disabilities.

Why do you need to Endure?

To successfully endure a pain or situation or event or person, it is nice to have a set goal before you or a focus of what you intend to achieve with your endurance, remembering the saying, no pain no gain. Mothers who get pregnant endure the pains and challenges of the pregnancy trusting God that at the end they will have a living baby or babies. Athletes who train in the rain and sunshine, good or bad weather have a hope of getting the medal at the end of their competition. Whatever the goal, we need to endure.

Time to run or Endure:

There is a time to use God's wisdom and flee rather than endure and suffer or lose one's life. Joseph and Samson were both exposed to wicked women who tormented them for a period of time. Joseph was wise to flee from an ungodly act; thereby refusing to sin against God and Potiphar and, though it landed him in the prison, it eventually led to his promotion as Egypt's first Prime Minister. He could have given in to Mrs. Potiphar's demands and avoided her torments but that decision would only have produced sin in his life, at the same time short-circuiting his destiny in God! Joseph did the wise thing in the circumstances – he chose to flee [*Genesis 39:1-21, 41:14-46*]. Samson on the other hand endured what he should not have allowed in the first instance, and this invariably led to his death [*Judges 16:1-30*].

Does endurance pay, why or why not?

Endurance that leads to someone achieving their positive goal or dream pays, just like the case of Joseph but endurance that endangers life, terminates destiny, aborts dreams like that of Samson does not pay off in the end and should not be tolerated.

Rewards of Endurance:

Positive endurance brings achieving one's goal in life which might in turn provide financial/ social/ emotional/ psychological/ professional stability.

Negative endurance if care is not taken leads to destruction and death.

What are you willing to Endure and why?

As an example, I am willing to write into the night – early hours of the morning – for the sake of the lives that will be blessed from the writings and the name of the Lord that will be glorified.

Those That Can Help Us Endure A Situation Or Pain Positively:
- God especially through His word and the Holy Spirit.
- Church/home group where people come round you to help and/or encourage you.

ENDURANCE

- Good Godly music / counselling.
- Undivided focus and,
- God-fearing friends and family - Biological or and Spiritual.

Exercise:

❖ Identify things that you should endure.
❖ Identify things that you should not endure.
❖ Should you be in a position or relationship that you should not endure, seek Godly counsel.

** Group coordinators should provide confidential same sex counselling and seek for help if and where needed.

Prayer Points:

God help me to know what I should endure and what I should not endure.

God grant me the grace to endure what You want me to endure.

Father, help me to run away from all that I should not be enduring.

ENDURANCE

FORGIVENESS

"It is in forgiving others that we also receive forgiveness from God."

"Forgive us our sins/ trespasses as we forgive those that trespass against us" [Luke 11:4]

Question For Consideration/ Discussion:
1. What is it?
2. Who do we need to forgive?
3. How often do we need to forgive others?
4. Are there some unpardonable sins?
5. Why do we need to forgive?
6. What if the person(s) is no more or I can't get to talk to the person(s)?
7. To forgive and forget, is it really possible?
8. Results of forgiveness and un-forgiveness.

What is Forgiveness?

Forgiveness means pardon, to have pity on someone or something, show mercy or grant amnesty or exonerate someone/something or to let go of an offender without any charges or punishment.

Who do we need to Forgive?

We need to forgive anyone who has offended us, including sometimes, our family members, associates and friends and ourselves for our misbehaviours – calculated and otherwise.

How often do we need to Forgive?

Daily and as often we get offended, irrespective of who did what to us, why, when, where and how?

Forgiveness should be a part of us just like our breathing. So long as we are human beings, we will continue to have the people/ things offending us. We must learn to forgive and move on in life. For some atrocities done to you many years ago, you may need to seek for Godly counselling and His divine protection. Jesus said we are to forgive anyone that offends us seventy times seven times per day, in other words,

God expects you to forgive every offense on a daily basis. That is why He says the sun should not set on your anger!

Are there some Unpardonable Sins?

There is one as far as I know. That is the sin against the Holy Spirit and the Bible says it cannot be forgiven. Bible scholars have understood it to mean ascribing the works of the Holy Spirit to the devil. You may want to check it out – Matthew 12:31; 1 John 5:16. For as long as Jesus died on the cross for mankind, He loves you and I and paid the full price of sin – my own and yours. He forgives each one who comes to Him with a repentant heart.

Why do we need to Forgive?

We need to forgive because Jesus said so, un-forgiveness also makes the person not to receive from the Lord, it exposes us to satanic attacks and influences, it is the reason for many diseases including some that are incurable and some deaths. Un-forgiveness has a way of releasing slow toxin within the body of the one who refuses to forgive. It is not worth it. Un-forgiveness produces bitterness in the heart of the one who refuses to forgive and it has been medically proven to have adverse effects on one's health.

What if the person(s) is no more or I can't get to talk to the person(s)?

An elderly minister once suggested that should this be the case, you should get two chairs in one room. You sit on one of the chairs and imagine the other person on the other chair. Pour out all your feelings and conclude by saying you forgive that person for all the hurts not so much that they deserve it but that it is God's commandment to you to forgive them.

To Forgive and Forget, is it really possible for anybody?

Some people are able to forget but for some it is not so easy. What is important is that once you truly forgive, when the thoughts about the person or incidence come up, you no longer have those bad, ugly feelings, you are able to talk about it without negative emotional eruptions.

Results of forgiveness	Results of un-forgiveness
You receive God's forgiveness	You lose God's forgiveness
Peace within yourself	Lack of peace
Answered prayers	Hindered prayers
Good health	Ill health and/or death

FORGIVENESS

Exercise:

- ❖ Identify times that you have been unable to forgive.
- ❖ How has this affected your relationship with God, that person/s and others?
- ❖ Given that you knew then what you know now about the situation, would you consider forgiving those who hurt you and forgive yourself?
- ❖ Search the Bible and find two scriptures that can help you to forgive. Memorise these scriptures and always quote it to Satan when he brings that situation up.
- ❖ Seek Godly counselling today if you are struggling to forgive.
- ❖ Remember to err is human but to forgive is divine.
- ❖ Remember a good antidote for un-forgiveness is a heart that focuses on and praises God.

*** Group coordinators should provide confidential same sex counselling and seek help if and where needed.*

PRAYER POINTS:

Lord, help me to forgive those who have hurt and abused me.

Lord, please forgive me, my family and community for our many sins.

Grant unto me Your divine peace of mind and a thankful heart always.

FORGIVENESS

GIVING

"He/she who cannot receive should not give"
"What you do not have, you cannot give"

"Give and it shall be given to you, good measure, pressed down, shaken together and running over will God make men to give unto your bosom." [Luke 6:38]

Question For Consideration/ Discussion:
1. What is it?
2. Who do we need to give to?
3. How often do we need to give to others?
4. Why do we need to give?
5. What can you give?
6. Is it wrong for one to receive gifts/blessings?
7. Results of giving?

What is Giving?

It is a charitable or philanthropic act, to be generous, open-handed, being bountiful or benevolent.

Who do we need to Give to?

We need to give first to God, the Giver of all, those who are in need who could be people we know or don't directly know, people around us or far away from us as in the foreign/mission fields and equally we need to give to ourselves and family.

How often do we need to Give to others?

As often as the Lord lays it on our heart and as often as there is a need around us for which we are in a position to help.

Why do we need to Give?

Giving is one of the attributes of God. When we give we are like our heavenly father who gives His best and all. Giving allows us to be a blessing and gives opportunity for God to bless us. River Jordan and the Dead Sea in Israel both have the same source but River Jordan is a blessing as it flows, giving life to man and other creatures whilst the Dead Sea has no living organism in it simply because it takes without giving.

What can you Give?

What we give will depend on what we have, who we are giving to and what is needed at the time. We could give to God our lives as in accepting Jesus as our Lord and Saviour and asking Him to be our Lord, we could give to God our time in serving Him and His people, we could give to God our talents in blessing Him and being a blessing to His people, we could give to God our wealth and monetary possessions as we give our tithes and offerings.

What sort of offerings do you Give?

The worst or the best? The left over and the not-so-good or the very best and choicest? It is not uncommon for some people to put into the offering bowl the most crumbled, barely readable monetary note, empty envelopes, damaged coins/money, pennies and foreign moneys that are of no value in that country. You may fool others and yourself but certainly not God. Whatsoever a man sows that he shall surely reap! This should make us to be more careful with what we give to God and our attitude in giving.

To people we could give our time, prayers, resources and required support. To ourselves we owe an environment of peace, love, generosity to ourselves whether anyone else is generous to us or not. We need to give time for ourselves and to prayers. Our attitude towards giving is as important, if not more than our gifts, especially giving towards the things of God. A wrong attitude may actually negate our gifts if care is not taken.

Giving should be done in line with God's word. Any giving that is done outside of God's word is not pure and can never be acceptable by God! For instance, you cannot give to God, money that is stolen. Likewise, be careful and weary of people who demand sex from you as a proof of your love to them. True love will wait till you are legally married before engaging in a sexual relationship with you.

Is it wrong for one to receive Gifts/Blessings?

Whilst the Bible teaches that it is more blessed to give than to receive, the Bible never says it is wrong to receive. Many believers are good at giving but not good at receiving. The

GIVING

Holy Spirit once said to me, 'he/she who is not fit to receive is not fit to give'. We must however be careful of what we receive and from whom and for what reason we receive gifts. Corruption within the society stems from giving and receiving bribes therefore both parties are dishonest before God and man and often can't say or abide by the truth.

When a man lavishes so much material wealth on another person especially on the person who is not in need, there is need to take a step back to check for any ulterior motives behind the giving before accepting such gifts, especially if the receiver is of the opposite sex. Many young people especially from poor homes or those who are greedy of wealth from wealthy homes have died while many more are dying unnecessarily from incurable or deadly sexually inflicted diseases contacted from trading their bodies for material wealth of perishable nature e.g. a mobile phone, some cash, clothes, cars etc and in the process they have caught incurable deadly diseases, some assaulted and killed.

In May 2009, American Online (AOL) news reported the case of an eighteen year old Romanian lady who sold her virginity to an Italian businessman for about $14,000! This is disheartening and should be discouraged because no matter how much the money is or how valuable the gift is that is received from such trade-offs, they are perishable but the effect on the human spirit, soul and body is for a lifetime and sometimes eternal!

Sometimes we are unable to receive out of pride. We think that will be-little us before the giver, and sometimes it is because we are not sure of the reason for the gift. At other times too, we are unable to receive because we feel we are better off in many ways than the giver. But this is not a good reason for not receiving. It is said that it is not so much the gift or the personality of the giver but the heart with which the gift is given. Remember the widow's mite? She gave the least in terms of amount, and her personality was nothing to be reckoned with in the midst of all the wealthy and influential people but Jesus said she her gift was the greatest because she gave her all.

It is said that you can give without loving but you cannot genuinely love without giving. There is need also to watch how we give. There is no gain or reward in giving to humiliate the other party or giving to ridicule the other person.

Results of Giving

Not only is there is a joy that accompanies giving with a right attitude, there is happiness knowing that your gift has gone to meet somebody else's needs. God is truly a rewarder and

GIVING

in due time will multiply unto the giver greater than that gift. Giving to God the rightful offering /sacrifice stopped the plaque during the reign of King David, however David said he would not give to God what has cost him nothing [2 Samuel 24:1-25 especially verse 24]. What has your giving cost you? Missing a meal? Not buying the new outfit / stereo etc? A wise man once said what you give to God does not leave your life but it goes into your future.

Exercise:

- ❖ Identify the best gift you have ever received.
- ❖ Identify the best gift you have ever given and the cost to you.
- ❖ How do you feel when you give especially something that someone else needs?
- ❖ Do you have a problem in being generous to others? If yes why is that?
- ❖ Are you a generous giver or not, and why?

Prayer Points:

Lord, teach me how and help me to be a giver of good gifts.

Lord, please enrich me so that I might be a generous giver that You intend me to be.

Father please grant me the seed that I can sow.

GIVING

HUMILITY

"My promotion lies in my humility and hard work"

"Humble yourself in the sight of the Lord, and He shall lift you up." [James 4:10].

Questions For Consideration/ Discussion:
1. What is it?
2. Why the need for humility?
3. Before whom do we need to be humble?
4. Who needs to be humble?
5. What humility is not.
6. Results of being humble.

What is It?

Humility is an attitude of a person being humble, modest, unassuming nature and meek. Such a person may or may not be shy.

Why the need for Humility?

Many people cannot tolerate a proud or boastful person. Humility is a good asset to being able to get along with God and people affably. A humble person is more likely to acknowledge God as the source of his/her outstanding achievement and be modest about it whilst a proud person is more likely to claim personal glory for same. God loves to work with and through humble people than otherwise.

Before whom do we need to be Humble and Why?

Humility before God is paramount if we want Him to bless and use us. God resists the proud. God is sovereign, the Creator and Sustainer of all creation including man. He knows the end before the beginning, His eyes see us all at the same time, He sees through us, into us, before us, beyond us and after us. He watches over His Words to perform in our lives and in the world, He knows all things and can do all

HUMILITY

things. He created from nothing, all things the world inclusive, through His spoken words. He is love and He loves us just as we are now without one plea! His love searches for us in our sins, weaknesses, rebellion against Him and destruction. He hears and speaks all languages, human, animals, birds and He communicates with all of His creation. There is nothing that we have that He did not give to us, nothing that we will ever become without Him or His knowledge, nowhere to hide from His presence. He deserves our praise and worship and we need to be humble before Him.

Humility before our parents, those who are older than us or in authority over us is essential to achieving our goals/aims in life. These people may not have as much education or wealth as us but they certainly have more experience than us or have been in that place or office longer than us so that we can tap into their wealth of knowledge to help us where we are and to help us become who God created us to be. This is important as it helps us to avoid the problems of life which makes many to stumble and prevents them from achieving their life goals. Some out of pride have died an early death.

Humility before our peers and those who are less privileged than us gives us a good aura and creates favour for us, acceptability and peace which when used positively contributes to our success. There is a wise saying that you should be mindful of those at the bottom of the ladder when you are climbing up for you will meet them on your way down too.

Who needs to be Humble?

Every one of us needs to be humble irrespective of our achievements, wealth, age, race and status. Leadership is about service to people. A humble person is more likely to want to serve others than being served.

What Humility is not:

Humility is not foolishness, stupidity, imprudence, idiocy or silliness. One can be humble without being stupid, silly, proud or foolish.

Results of Humility:

In good and God's time a humble person gets promoted and honoured. A humble person tends to attract favour and God is able to use and bless such person. Examples are Moses, the most humble man in the world and Jesus in Philippians 2: 9-11. Humility is a key to successful leadership.

EXERCISE:

- ◈ Identify times that you have not been humble and to whom.
- ◈ What has your lack of humility cost you?
- ◈ Identify steps that you can take to make you a more humble person in life.
- ◈ Are humility and stupidity related? – NO!

PRAYER POINTS:

God teach me and help me to be humble.

Help me Lord to be humble in life.

Lord may I never be proud in my daily walk.

'Let's Reason Together ...Youths' A-Z

MY PERSONAL NOTES

INTEGRITY

"Let your 'yes' be 'yes' and 'nay' be 'nay".

"Ye are the light of the world. A city that is set on a hill cannot be hid." [Matthew 5:14]

Questions For Consideration/ Discussion:
1. What is it?
2. Why the need for integrity?
3. Where is integrity needed today?
4. Results of good integrity.

What is Integrity?

Integrity is an attitude that shows up as honest, reliable, dependable, truthful, honourable, veracity and upright. In other words it means a person with integrity is one who can be trusted to keep his/her words no matter what, a person of substance, a person who is reliable and truthful.

Why the need for Integrity?

The world today is full of many dishonest, deceitful and wicked people. The world's problems can be traced to many who have been or are being or will be dishonest. Some government officials and politicians cannot be trusted to keep their election promises. Some parents, friends, family members, business associates can't either. Some friends cannot be trusted with one's spouse or children as they will abuse them sexually or otherwise. Each person will stand before God some day and to Him alone we shall give the account of how we spent our lives. As Christians we are to be people of integrity if we are to be the salt of the earth and light of the world, drawing and pointing men and women to meet with Jesus Christ at the cross.

INTEGRITY

Where is Integrity needed today?

Integrity is needed everywhere, every time and wherever mankind is found. To be a person of integrity you need to make up your mind, God helping you, to stay focussed on God and be who He would have you be in all circumstances. Let me assure you that anyone whom God will use will at some point have his/her integrity tested and exposed.

Contentment is crucial to this principle. Joseph was a man of great integrity. He had purposed in his heart not to sin against God and his master in spite of his master's wife wooing him and pestering him *[Genesis 39:1-15]*. Opportunities and temptations will come your way to have a fast, quick fling or affair, take the short cut in your studies or vocation, or do something contrary to the will of God but which is possibly acceptable as a societal norm. What will you do when such an occasion arises?

You might say but Joseph was jailed in spite of his so-called integrity, but while that might be true, the Lord used his stay in the prison as His stepping stone to becoming Egypt's first Prime Minister. You may get into trouble in spite of your integrity, nevertheless God will use such problems to promote you into your destiny.

Results of Integrity:

Being a person of integrity attracts unquantifiable rewards e.g. peace of mind, favour with God and man, lack of fear of the press, unimaginable respect and trust within the community, ability to become who God has designed you to be, being a blessing to your generation and others to come, which in turn brings Glory to God. .

INTEGRITY

EXERCISE:

- ❖ Ask your best friend to tell you if you are a person of integrity and why or why not.
- ❖ What makes you say 'yes' when you actually mean 'no'?
- ❖ Have you ever been punished for your integrity? – share the story with the group if you can.
- ❖ What has your lack of integrity cost you or your family?
- ❖ Identify reasons why you are not a person of integrity and what you can do to overcome this.
- ❖ Ask God for forgiveness where you have erred and for His grace to become a person of integrity.
- ❖ Identify a mentor who can monitor your integrity and to whom you can be accountable.
- ❖ Contact this person today.

PRAYER POINTS:

Lord, forgive me for not paying attention to my integrity.

Lord, please help me to be a person of integrity.

Lord, please surround me with men and women of integrity.

'Let's Reason Together ...Youths' A-Z

MY PERSONAL NOTES

JUSTICE

JUSTICE

"Righteousness exalts a nation"

"Defend the poor and fatherless: do justice to the afflicted and needy"
[Psalm 82:3].

Questions For Consideration/Discussion:
1. What is it?
2. Why the need for it?
3. Where is Justice needed today.
4. Results of Justice.

What is Justice?

Justice is the ability of a person or system to be fair. In other words, it means to have a fair dealing. It may also mean impartiality, honesty, integrity.

The need for Justice:

Many in the world today are not being treated fairly or rightly, they are denied their rights, entitlements and privileges sometimes because they are ignorant of their rights and have no one to tell them and at other times because they are incapable of defending themselves and/or have no one to help them.

Some are denied their entitlements because of their skin colour or because of an ailment or deformity and others because of their political party, faith, gender, age, poverty, or status.

Where is Justice needed today?

Justice is needed in every area of human life or endeavour. There is need to defend human rights everywhere in every aspect of human existence – in schools, offices, homes, prisons, religious houses, across nations and communities, hospitals, even in the grave yards! There are many people across the globe who are hurting and demoralised simply because they have been denied access to their rights by a few people who are more privileged. Some have been confined to mental homes as a result of their rights being denied and others have turned their anger on bitterness on God by denying Him! It is very saddening when one is rejected on the basis of injustice, or to have one's rights denied deliberately.

Results of Justice.

When justice is executed, the people are happy, there is peace in the land, the government or group or person gains the confidence of the people being served. Every man is equal before the Almighty God, everyman deserves to be heard, respected, valued and treated equally. There is no race that God made to be superior or inferior to another. Every human being is unique and individually talented. We need to learn to appreciate and celebrate our differences. Our strength, uniqueness and individuality is in our differences.

Today, the world is crying out for justice, yet the Bible is full of principles that can guide us into knowing and exercising justice in our little ways. Study it, meditate on it and purpose never to cheat anyone for any reason. God is the God of all men. He sees all things and can do all things.

TAKE TIME

Take time to admire
God's richness in every creature He made
Though little, seemingly insignificant or even magnificent
Yet every creature speaks volumes of God's beauty and love.

Take time to fellowship
For Christ's presence you will experience with others there
Sharing the Word and bread
Being richly blessed whilst also becoming a blessing.

Take time to listen
Best communicators are very good at listening
Listen to the needs around
And what more, to the silent still voice of the Holy Spirit.

Take time to love
For that is the nature of our Father in heaven
Costly as it may be sometimes
It is the only gift that never fails eternally whilst others cease.

JUSTICE

Take time to pray
For in it lies divine power and revelation
Christ is our unique example
A prayerless Christian is a powerless one.

Take time to read the scriptures (God's word)
For therein lies light to your ways and lamp to your feet
Time consuming, as it may seem
Therein lies a balanced picture of God's purpose for all.

Take time to reflect
On God's answers to your prayers and the many blessings
Refreshing and reassuring
Your courage renewed and faith strengthened for the future.

Take time to serve
For in lowly service lies true and good leadership
And what more thereafter
There is a great reward for all your humble service.

Take time to share the gospel
For that is the great commission of Christ to all believers
As He ascended to heaven
Each addition to the fold causes great rejoicing in heaven.

Take time to sing
For it is the only occupation there in heaven
A good practice here
Gives a foretaste of the wonderful eternity yet to come.

Take time to visit others
For at the judgment you will be rewarded
And whilst you are away
Devil cannot meet you at home to tempt, use or destroy you.

Take time to write
Encouraging others in this heaven bound earthly pilgrimage
And when you are no more
It will be a Godly legacy to many generations yet to come.

Take time today friend
Amidst your very busy schedule, duties and appointments
Go out of your way
Do that which for so long you have neglected in your Christian life.

Take time to encourage others
For as you do, you too get encouraged
The measure with which you mete to others
Will one day be used for you.

JUSTICE

Take time to encourage others
In their Christian walk in life
No believer can make it to heaven by himself
Without other people's Godly influence and encouragements.
©O.Ola-Ojo 14/02/93

EXERCISE:

◈ What does justice means to you as a person?
◈ Identify some injustices in our society/community today?
◈ Why are the poor often denied access to justice?
◈ What can you do as a person/group to address the prevailing identified injustice in our community?
◈ Identify some individuals or groups who can help bring justice to the poor in your community e.g. civil rights group and contact them as a group today.

PRAYER POINTS:

Pray for justice to be done in our Country and land.

Pray that God will use you and others in your generation to defend the poor and vulnerable.

Ask God to help you obey His laws and be a law abiding citizen in Jesus name.

JUSTICE

KNOWLEDGE

"I know my God and I shall be strong and do exploits".

"My people are destroyed for lack of knowledge…
[Hosea 4:6]

Questions For Consideration/ Discussion:
1. What is it?
2. Why the need for it?
3. Where is it needed today?
4. Results of good knowledge.

What is Knowledge?

Many words can be used to describe it including awareness, data, facts, familiarity, information and understanding. There is good knowledge that brings about solutions to problems, answers to questions and good living and there is bad knowledge that seeks to and actually does lure some into sin, sickness, poverty and death. Any knowledge that increases your value as a person and enhances yourself worth without damaging others around you is good knowledge. Any knowledge that destroys others around you, decreases or denies your value and self worth, diminishes or puts you down either in your words or actions, demoralises you, leads and lures you to sin, sickness and ultimate death, farther away from God and His people is bad knowledge.

Why the need for it?

For the lack of knowledge, my people perish says the Bible. There is a solution to every problem in the world that anyone can come across provided that person has the right knowledge, first of the problem, and next, of where to seek for its solution, doing so without any delay or procrastination. That takes knowledge to do. The world as God created it is without any known human end, vast, beyond description and measurement, full of resources and mysteries. The best of science and technology is just scratching its surface.

We need Godly knowledge to have dominion over the world, to understand God and all that He created, to understand our assignment and how to successfully go about it.

Where is it needed today?

The whole world is seeking for one form or another form of knowledge that will make life better, easier and cheaper so as to accomplish much more in a given time frame with the least resources.

There is so much to know about the challenges/ obstacles that daily or regularly challenge us. The world is seeking for spiritual, social and financial knowledge, an understanding of so many things. In each field, there are lots of things to be discovered to make mankind's life better.

"The fear of the Lord is the beginning of wisdom/knowledge" [Proverbs 1:7], "receive my instruction and not silver and knowledge rather than choice gold" [Proverbs 8:10]

Knowledge is power. Those who have knowledge often rule the world. You need to spend quality time reading and researching to acquire knowledge. Readers often are the leaders because they have the knowledge.

Where can you get it today?

Knowledge could be obtained from schools, books, media generally and specifically, internet, colleagues, older or more experienced folks, or from those who are better educated in the field for which you seek specific knowledge. However knowledge that is obtained from God, His written or spoken words is the best for many reasons some of which include:

The best of mankind is grossly limited but God is not.
God created the world and all that it contains; He is also in control of every situation but man is not!

God is so meticulous that He knows and is aware of everything going on in life. He alone knows the number of hair on our heads. No science or technology can do that!

God in His sovereignty knows the end before the beginning of any matter, He knows everyone and has ordained every day of your life. Man only knows the present second he/she is in.

God is never caught by surprise whereas man often is, if not always.

KNOWLEDGE

Every career, constitution, formula, life scenario has a precedence in the Bible if only you can read it e.g.

WHAT	REFERENCE
Plantation/gardening	Genesis 1 –2
Anaesthesia before surgery	Genesis 2:21
Organ donation/plastic surgery	Genesis 2:22
Law and punishment for its disobedience	Genesis 2-3
Relationship/marriage	Genesis 2: 18- 25
Family	Genesis 4
Murder and God's punishment	Genesis 4
Registry of birth and death	Genesis 5
Ark/ship construction	Genesis 6-8
Zoology	Genesis 6-8
Round the world on a ship	Genesis 6-9
Weather forecast	Genesis 8:7-13, 9 :11-18
Brewery and effect of wine on man	Genesis 9: 20 – 27
Brick making, city construction	Genesis 11
Organisation, Disorganisation and multiple languages	Genesis 11
Travelling abroad	Genesis 12
War and rescue	Genesis 14
Priesthood and tithes	Genesis 14
Infertility	Genesis 15-16
God's covenant with man	Genesis 17

Circumcision /Covenant	Genesis 17: 1-13, 23- 27
Land owner	Genesis 17
Hospitality/guests	Genesis 18
Homosexuality and God's view on it	Genesis 18 -19
City destruction	Genesis 19
Linguistic	Genesis 19 -20
Incest	Genesis 19:30-38
Bareness in the palace	Genesis 20:17-18
Punishment for taking another man's wife	Genesis 20:1-18
Overcoming infertility – couple's way/Surrogacy	Genesis 21:1-8
Oasis in the desert/God answers a child's prayers	Genesis 21:9-20
Resolving infertility – God's way and time	Genesis 21
Sacrificial lamb	Genesis 22
Funeral/cemetery	Genesis 23
Expensive wedding	Genesis 24
Nurse	Genesis 24
Widower getting married	Genesis 25:1-6
Family business/working for uncle	Genesis 29
Stealing and its consequences	Genesis 31:26-35
Change of name	Genesis 35
Slavery	Genesis 37
Sexual temptation and false accusation	Genesis 39

KNOWLEDGE

Right/good presentation	Genesis 41:8-14
Dream interpretation	Genesis 40-41
Massive food preservation/storage/food dunes	Genesis 41:46-49
International trading	Genesis 42
Family reunion after 22 years	Genesis 45, 46:28 34
King owning all the land, cattle and people	Genesis 47:13-22
20% Taxation	Genesis 47:23-26
Clan migration abroad	Genesis 46-47
Man with only a child	Genesis 46:23
Father's prophecy and blessing	Genesis 48-49
Father's will	Genesis 48:21-22
International mourning and burial	Genesis 50
Forced labour	Exodus 1:8-14
Midwives	Exodus 1:15-21
Baby given for adoption	Exodus 2:1-6
Paid Nanny	Exodus 2:7-10

This is just to mention a few examples.

Only God can give a lasting/permanent solution to any problem –personal or communal – not man.

Results of Knowledge:

Good knowledge brings about solutions to problems, answers to questions and good living. Bad knowledge lures some into sin, sickness, poverty and death.

Every form of knowledge must be assessed to identify/sift the bad from the good one. When you hear about God without putting what you hear in your heart, you only have head knowledge but when you put God and His words into your heart, heaven is your limit. Knowledge will uplift you from nobody into somebody, from ignorance into awareness in Jesus' name. Academic knowledge is good but knowledge of God is best.

KNOWLEDGE

Exercise:

- Identify areas where you need more knowledge.
- Where can you get this knowledge?
- Take steps today to pursue seeking that knowledge.
- 'Knowledge is power'. What does this mean to you?
- How knowledgeable are you in the Word of God?

Prayer Points:

Lord, please grant me the knowledge for my assignment in life.

Lord, grant me your divine knowledge.

Lord, please help me to spend quality time at Your feet learning from You.

'Let's Reason Together ...Youths' A-Z

LOVE

"Love God and love others as yourself".

"For God so loved the world that He gave His only begotten Son that whosoever believes in Him should not perish but have everlasting life" [John 3:16].

Questions For Consideration/ Discussion:
1. What is love?
2. Who or what do we tend to love?
3. What are the types of love?
4. Where is love needed today?
5. How can we show our love?

What is Love?

Love can be described as affection for someone or something, to be keen on someone or something, worship, adore or care for someone or something, be devoted to someone or something, or to find someone or something irresistible.

Who or what do we tend to Love?:

God, our parents, friends, people, toys such as our bikes, cars, game boy, pet, work or career, our spouse, our children, job, vacation, our achievements etc.

What are the types of Love?

Agape
This is God's unfailing love to mankind, it is an unconditional love; it continues to seek after mankind, wooing us to Himself 24 x 7. It is a love that a single person or the whole community cannot deny or ignore; it is a love that can never be parallel or equalled. It is love that accepts the one being loved unconditionally. It is the love of the Creator/Maker towards His creatures.

Eros
Otherwise referred to as erotic love, it is the love that is based mostly on the feelings of a man and a woman in love, feelings that are many times sensual and/or conditional. Oftentimes, it is lust that is presented as love and sometimes the lust manifests in sexual satisfaction/ gratification of one person at the expense of the other.

Philia/Filia
This is love for a brother or sister i.e. siblings or family members.

Where is Love needed today?

Everywhere there is life, there is need for love. The world is the way it is today due to lack of love for God and fellow human beings. People tend to love money, pets, and lifeless things than God or fellow human beings. Where there is true love, there will be respect for human life and peace. True love always gives.

How can we show our Love?

TO GOD
Give your life to Jesus Christ, develop and maintain un-interrupted fellowship with God with the help of the Holy

Spirit, for we were all created to worship Him. Obey God's commandments, read and meditate on His Words in the Bible, sing songs unto Him, serve God and His people and love all that God loves and vice versa.

OTHERS

Respect them and treat them as God's children too, appreciate them and love them with the love of the Lord but not more than yourself. Don't try to buy love or affection whether of the same or opposite sex; it does not pay or last and no matter what, you will always have to pay more price each time to gain the same effect or affection. If you think by kissing, petting or sleeping with another person you have conquered their love, you need to think twice for often such people will classify you as cheap, unsatisfying, and untrustworthy and not befitting their status etc. and what started as love often ends up in bitterness, separation, anger, infection with sexually transmitted diseases, unwanted pregnancy or abortion etc. A person who loves you is the one that waits, properly marries you (in accordance with your culture, belief or religion) before making any sexual advances to you.

'Love is very fragile, handle with care and prayer'
'Love is very fragile, prayerfully handle with care'
'Love is very fragile, carefully handle with prayer'

LOVE

Touch Someone Today

There are five senses in a human being
The sense of sight, hearing and smelling
That of tasting and touching
Through which messages are received and relayed.

However, the power of touching is so real
Whilst others could be easily mistaken or unnoticed
That of touch cannot be mistaken or easily forgotten
Especially in times of great needs of man.

No wonder the Rabbi begged Jesus for a touch
On His little daughter who has just died at home
Great was his faith in Jesus' healing power
That would raise the dead girl just by mere touching.

The unnamed woman with the issue of blood
Had suffered for twelve years in the hands of all
Despised, rejected, weak, feeble, faint and weary
She sought for complete healing from Jesus Christ.

Aware of the difficulties to be encountered
She was contented only with touching Jesus' garment
For she believed that would procure the desired healing
What a joy as her faith was honoured and recognised.

'Stir up the gift of God', Paul admonished Timothy
Which had been given to you when hands were laid
Upon your head, and be no longer afraid of anything
But filled with power, love and a strong mind.

Stop underestimating that touch of the Almighty God
Upon you dearly friend through God's messengers
Begin today to flow in God's mighty power
Unto every being you come in contact with.

Be kind to give a friendly touch dear friend
To that person you know needs your help now
To that very sick child and the worried parent
Let them feel God's, love and power through your touch.

God is able to bring about the miracle through you
Identify with that person's problem today
As you reach out to touch him and the need
If anything dear friend, touch someone today.
©O.Ola-Ojo 8/7/90

YOURSELF

The least you owe yourself is love. You can only give what you have. If you don't love yourself how then can you truly love others? Irrespective of what your skin colour is, achievements, physical appearance etc. you owe yourself love. If you do not love yourself, the tendency is for you to mistreat or abuse yourself, or allow others to do so to you at your expense and for their own fun or enjoyment. When it becomes obvious that you don't love yourself, you can be sure others too will not make efforts to love you. Appreciate God for your looks for many others are yearning and praying for that body part/family/background/ talent you are currently despising. It doesn't matter whether you are short or tall, thin or fat, able or disabled etc. God made you wonderfully and complexly and more so there is no true 100 % duplicate of yourself *[Psalms 139:13-16]*.

You are uniquely unique as a man of God often says. You may not love all your actions e.g. stealing, lying, laziness etc. but still love yourself and in the name of the Lord, prayerfully work on your weaknesses. My question to you is: "Do you love yourself?"

Do You Love Yourself?

Love your neighbour as yourself
Is the Biblical injunction to all
But the question comes to mind
Do you love yourself dear friend?

Many want to love their neighbours
As themselves many a times
Yet they do not love themselves
Enough to transfer this love to others.

You have been hearing the salvation message
Over and over again from many people
Do you love yourself enough to accept
Jesus Christ as your Lord and Saviour?

Do you love yourself as a child in the home
Respecting your parents and those older than you?
Do you fulfil all your family obligations
To merit a long life full of blessing?

Do you love yourself as a student
In your attendance at lectures?
Is your submission of assignments timely?
How hard do you study for examinations?

Do you love yourself in your marital relationship?
Is your marriage based on God's principles?
Is it based on monogamy and permanency?
Is it based on fidelity and love?

LOVE

God has blessed you with riches and talents
Do you love yourself enough to give them back to Him
As you give willingly to the spread of the gospel?
And wisely utilise your talents to bless mankind?

Do you love yourself in yourself evaluations?
Are your confessions negative or positive?
Is your thought true, pure, lovely, good and right?
How much do you pray for yourself?

Self is one's greatest enemy
The flesh lusteth (lusting) against the spirit
What you want to do that you don't do
What you don't want is what you do.

'Charity begins at home' is the saying of the wise
Start to love yourself from now
In your thoughts, utterances and actions
Then loving your neighbour will be easy for you.
[Philippians 4:8, Matthew 19:19 & Romans 8:21-25].
© Ola - Ojo. 06/04/88.

Results of True Love

When you truly love God, your relationship with Him will be meaningful and fruitful and He rewards those who diligently seek Him. When you love your family and siblings, you are likely to have it reciprocated to you, have peace with them and receive support from them. When you fall in love and marry according to God's will you will enjoy marital blessings. When you love yourself, as you should, loving others will not be difficult.

'True love always seeks to give and share'. You may want to refer to *'12 Healthy Attitudes Towards Myself'* shared earlier too. See page 30.

LOVE

Exercise:

❖ Identify those you are supposed to love.
❖ Who among them do you find difficult to love and why?
❖ Have you ever loved your neighbours than yourself? When and how?
❖ How can you love yourself better from now?
❖ When are you going to start loving yourself?

Prayer Points:

Lord, please help me to love You with all I have.

Lord, please teach me how best I can love myself.

Lord help me to be a example of Your love to all I meet.

'Let's Reason Together ...Youths' A-Z

MY PERSONAL NOTES

MIRACLES

"Miracles are still an every time occurrence with God".

"With God nothing shall be impossible" [Luke 1:37].

Questions For Consideration/Discussion
1. What is a miracle?
2. Is there a need for any miracle today?
3. Where are miracles needed today?
4. Results of Miracles.
5. Are there still miracles today as in the days of the Bible?

What is a Miracle?

A miracle is an observable fact that is a wonder, an experience that is phenomenal, a happening that is undisputable, a positive incident or event that beats any man's imagination/expectation, an unnatural occurrence that is beyond any human expertise, a divine or supernatural intervention, just to mention a few.

Is there a need for any Miracle today?

In our sophisticated world today, the need for miracles is as real and great as it was during the Bible times.

There are so many human needs as there were in times past, although in other dimensions. People are still falling sick, poor, uncomfortable, tormented, in despair and disarray. There is sin everywhere with its obvious repercussion; there are hopeless cases as they were in the times of Jesus and His disciples. If anything the world could do with much more miracles than those of the Bible times.

Where are Miracles needed today?

Wherever there is a need, there is the potential for a miracle to happen. In view of the fact that there is no man/human being without a challenge or need most of which cannot be resolved by each/that individual, it means everybody is or will be in need of a miracle once or more in their lifetime. Take for instance, money can buy medicine, Doctors and technology but money cannot buy good health. Beauty, charisma and connections can buy a relationship/or marriage but it cannot buy a truly happy, fulfilling marriage. Work and money can buy food but it cannot buy the ability to eat or digest it. Money can buy In-Vitro Fertilisation (IVF) technology and treatment but it cannot give a pregnancy or sustain one.

Miracles could be small or big, they are all from the same God. As small and as many times ignored, sleeping soundly and waking up are miracles and they are from God. Walking, breathing, talking, urinating, eating and doing all the ordinary things of life are miracles from God and it must be so acknowledged, especially when you think of more opportune, better-placed people who for reasons beyond their control cannot enjoy the same opportunities like yourself. Both the recipient and the Lord know the touch of faith.

Results of Miracles

Those who have experienced a miracle certainly know that there has been a supernatural occurrence even though they may not want to acknowledge God as the giver. Because of the sophistication of the West with modern technology, science and hospital facilities, oftentimes, some in the West find it difficult to acknowledge miracles and God the giver of miracles.

Are there still Miracles today as in the days of the Bible?

Yes and much more. However the media is many times silent about them or they may want to play it down to 'mother nature'. Other reasons for not hearing much about miracles include – unbelief in the Body of Christ, lack of knowledge of the same and available power in Jesus as in the days of old, not sharing the testimony of individual miracles experienced in the congregation of believers, not wanting to identify with Jesus Christ publicly or disclose our problems, sins or challenges from which we have had a breakthrough or miracle and most importantly ingratitude and pride towards God. Many even in the Body of Christ take God for granted assuming that these blessings including miracles are their right not privileges. There is a need to

MIRACLES

repent of this sin and to adjust our attitude in this regard. As we lift the name of Jesus higher in our testimonies, He is glorified and draws more people unto Himself. We retain our testimonies and miracles often as we testify and cover our testimonies in the blood of Jesus [Revelations 12:11a]. Thanking God for little blessings positions us for greater ones.

** *Please give room for people to share the testimonies about their miracles.*

Exercise:

- ❖ Miracles and magic are they the same? - NO
- ❖ Is the era of miracles gone since the Bible days?- NO
- ❖ Identify your most and least spectacular miracles.
- ❖ How much did you pay for your least experienced miracle?
- ❖ Thank God for these miracles and share the testimony with others.

Prayer Points:

Lord, please help me to see more of Your miracles moment by moment of everyday.

Lord, please make my life a miracle that will testify of Your goodness to the world around me and beyond.

Lord, grant me opportunities and the grace to testify of Your miracles daily.

MIRACLES

MY PERSONAL NOTES

NETWORKING

"Evil association corrupts good manners".

"He that walketh with wise men shall be wise: but a companion of fools shall be destroyed" [Proverbs 13:20]

Questions for Consideration/Discussion
1. What is it?
2. Why do we need to network?
3. Where do people get to network?
4. Who should you be networking with?
5. Is networking good for me?

Whatis It?

According to Encarta Dictionary English (U.K), it is the act of linking computers or the practice of gathering of contacts. For the purpose of this discussion, we shall consider networking as it relates to gathering of contacts.

Why do we need to Network?

Many people network to get access to job or business opportunities for now or later. For others it is a form of having informal relationships or friendships or catching up on old friendships such as school or work or house mates.

Where do people get to Network?

It could be done through the internet using facilities such as face book, twitter etc, or by attending events such as business meetings, social meetings, youth clubs, Sunday – school, holiday retreats etc.

NETWORKING

Who should you be Networking with?

Many people tend to have networks that will help with their jobs or profession or business. Others do social networking for making and keeping friends and old mates. There is a wise saying that each one of us is just four people away from the person who can help us have our breakthrough. Someone has what you are searching for in life, whatever it is. Someone knows perhaps another person who knows who is holding on to that which you are searching for.

Is Networking good for me?

This is a personal question best answered by you. However here are some questions or points to consider before you decide if it is good for you or not:

- Why do you want to do some networking?
- Who will you want to have network with?
- Which sites or events will you be attending?
- What proportion of your time do you intend to spend on networking?
- How will networking enhance you, your work or studies or business or otherwise?
- Will or has the networking enhance your relationship with God in line with the Bible or otherwise?

- Is the network helping you to be a better person or otherwise?
- Is the network fuelling your strengths or weakness?
- Is the network gradually luring or drawing you away from your family and friends?
- Is the network gradually grooming you for anything ungodly? If so, run as fast your legs can carry you.

Please note the following:

- Avoid spending all or most of your useful/productive time on networking – you need to develop yourself, career or job too.
- Avoid being a channel or receiver or giver of gossips and untold rumours.
- It is not advisable to date a person through social networking especially from the internet. Recently a pretty 17-year old girl was assaulted and murdered by the 33-year old man she dated on the internet in the UK. There are so many evil minded, wicked people who use social internet network sites to lure the unwearied, groom them and exploit them. May your case not be like that in Jesus' name.
- Will God be happy with your chosen network group or associates?

NETWORKING

- Please do not meet in person anyone you have dated or befriended through the internet by yourself alone and in a private or secluded place.
- Should you realise that you have joined the wrong network, repent and get out of it now that you still have your life and the time to do so.

*** Group coordinators should provide confidential same sex counselling and seek help if and where needed.*

EXERCISE:

◈ Share with the group how you network and why.
◈ Share your experience on networking.
◈ Will you recommend your type of networking to other friends? Why or why not?
◈ Are you able to share your faith with your group of network associates or friends if not why not?
◈ What benefits have you gained from your networking and at what cost to yourself?

PRAYER POINTS:

Lord, guide me into the right networks.

Lord, in your mercy help me to be focussed on my calling in life so that I might not be derailed through my social network.

Lord, please grant me the grace to represent You and all that You stand for in my networking.

NETWORKING

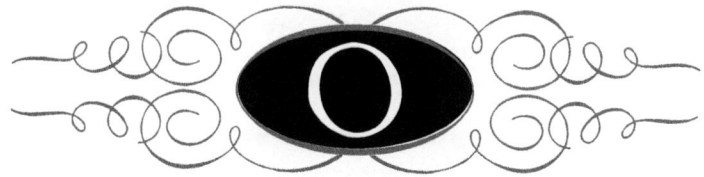

OATH

"Be a man or woman of your words"

"When thou vowest a vow unto God, defer not to pay it; for he hath no pleasure in fools: pay thou which thou hast vowed" [Ecclesiastes 5:4].

Questions for Consideration/ Discussion:
1. What is an oath?
2. Why do people make/swear to an oath?
3. Examples of oaths in the Bible.
4. Conditions for an oath.
5. Are all oaths good?
6. What to do if you want to end an ungodly oath.

What is an Oath?

It is a promise or vow or pledge between two or more people. It could also mean a covenant. In certain professions or for certain offices, you are expected to take an oath of the office e.g. Doctor's oath, President of a country takes the oath of office, witnesses take an oath in the court of law before testifying before the judge, etc.

Why do people make/swear to an Oath?

Oaths are made to protect each other's interest at all times and situations. It could also mean fighting and defending each other should there be need for it. It is always/mostly a lifelong contract/promise. It could be extended to unborn generations from all sides. It is a promise /vow/pledge that has to be made consciously and verbally with each party involved willing to abide by the terms of the oath, therefore an oath is binding on those who take it.

It could also be an expression of love for each other especially between a man and a woman. An oath can be taken verbally or in writing. Often when it is a relationship based oath it maybe sealed by a token which could be the exchange of gifts, blood/body fluid, bodily incisions, etc.

OATH

Examples of Oaths in the Bible

- God promised never to destroy the world with water again and gave mankind the rainbow as a token [Genesis 9:12 – 17].
- God and Abraham [Genesis 15 and 17:1-14].
- Abraham and Abimelech [Genesis 21:22 –34].
- Isaac and Abimelech [Genesis 26: 26 –35].
- Jacob vows to God [Genesis 28:10-22].
- Jacob and Laban [Genesis 31:43-55].
- David and Jonathan [1 Samuel 20: 4-23, 35 – 42].

Conditions for an Oath

People taking the oath must have similar interest and, they design and agree to the terms of the oath. They are mindful and watchful over each other to ensure that the terms of the oath are maintained. For some ungodly oaths, e.g. that of joining a cult, concoctions are prepared, each party's body is cut so that drops of blood from them is mixed with the concoctions before they drink it etc.

Are all Oaths good?

No, every oath that does not involve the Almighty God of the Bible is ungodly. Ungodly oaths that have to do with cults often involve the participants wearing certain outfits, meeting exclusively at odd times and places, may seal the oath with their blood, and they may not have respect for the lives of others. Such cults are not clubs or Churches that you can visit at your own discretion and leave when you like. They tend to instil in their members terrible fears that keep them bound to the cult by the oath they took. In certain cults, when the person that made the oath dies, at least one of the children will be expected to join them and continue in the cult. Some today are suffering as a result of oaths made by their forefathers. For such people, they need to take a Godly stand against their forefather's oath and remain in the Lord.

What to do if you want to end an ungodly Oath.

You need first to give your life to Jesus Christ and come under His covering and name. Confess to God your sin / mistake of joining an ungodly person or group in the days of your ignorance. Find Bible passages that will empower you over the attacks of Satan. Stay focussed on God, Jesus Christ and the blood He shed for you and on the Holy Spirit, the best Counsellor. You also need to banish all forms of fear, standing upon the written and spoken word of God for your life and, with your mouth denounce your relationship with the ungodly oath. You need to destroy any of the articles that links or binds you to the ungodly oath, stop attending their meetings and avoid going to places where other members can challenge you. It is also wise to identify a Godly mentor and prayer partner who will stand with you in this battle. Be honest and open with your mentor. Prepare for attacks in all forms but remember greater is He that lives in you now than the devil that is of the world.

EXERCISE:

❖ Have you entered into any ungodly oath? Seek for Godly counsel immediately.
❖ Write down at least two Bible passages that you will memorize and recite to yourself daily.
❖ What steps would you take to get out of an ungodly oath that you made by yourself or that which was made on your behalf? – identify the oath, confess your sins or that of your fore fathers to God in prayers, accept the Lordship of Jesus Christ, renounce the oath, seek for Godly deliverance and back up, walk in the light of God's words and principles etc.
❖ Choose a mentor who can correct and encourage you i.e. be accountable to someone e.g. your youth pastor or counsellor – you will need to open up to this mentor or counsellor so they can know where and how to help you.
❖ Ask God to give you a new set of godly friends.
❖ Get involved in the Church and youth dedicated activities.

** Group coordinators should provide confidential same sex counselling and seek help if and where needed.

OATH

PRAYER POINTS:

Lord, please deliver me from every ungodly oath that I might have taken in times past.

Lord, please deliver me from every ungodly oath of my forefathers which is now tormenting or negatively affecting me.

Lord, please grant me the grace and wisdom of God to know which oath to avoid and which oath to take and which oath to run away from.

'Let's Reason Together ...Youths' A-Z

MY PERSONAL NOTES

PRESENTATION

"People see me before they hear me or get to know me".

"Let not then your good be evil spoken of."
[Romans 14:16]

Questions For Consideration/Discussion
1. What is it?
2. Why is presentation important?
3. How to go about good presentation.
4. What contributes to good presentation?
5. Results of good presentation.
6. Results of bad presentation.
7. Has my presentation anything to do with my future?

What is It?

It is how a thing or person appears to or is perceived by the outside world. A good thing /person can be presented badly and vice versa. It is someone's first impression about a thing, person or place.

Why is Presentation important?

The agent of 'first impression' is as real today as it was in the Bible times. Presentation is about acceptance by others, peers, a person or persons in higher authority. Whilst not trying to be like the 'Jones' you need to begin to dress for where you intend to be. A common cliché says, dress the way you want to be addressed. David almost lost his opportunity to get into limelight because of his 'shepherd boy' appearance at the war front *[1 Samuel 17]*. Esther became the preferred virgin to replace Queen Vashti partly because of her appearances or presentation to the king. Of all the virgins, she was the only one who took counsel on what to wear for her night with the king. Some opportunities come once in a life time! Daniel and his friends were chosen partly because of their appearances for the kingly duties training [Daniel 1:4]. Joseph had to shave, possibly shower and change his clothes before appearing before Pharaoh

PRESENTATION

[Genesis 41:14]. Ruth had her appearance worked upon before presenting herself to rich Boaz *[Ruth 3:1-7]*.

Presentation is very important in many professions therefore their preferred uniform and code of conduct e.g. Navy, Police, Doctors, Nurses, Radiographers, various sports people, lawyers etc.

How to go about good Presentation:

- ❖ Learn to understand who you are, where you are going, who you are likely to meet and the preferred dress code or presentation code. Most kings and those in authorities will hardly look or have time or even allow a tattered dressed or uncultured, ill-mannered person in their presence no matter the anointing such a person carries. Most companies or individuals who bid for contracts etc. by competition will use their best human and technological resources for such.
- ❖ Depend on the Holy Spirit who created all and knows about all, to guide you in your selections of all presentation materials including what to wear on a daily basis.
- ❖ Seek Godly and professional advice like Esther if need be for often times you may not have the second chance to make a first impression.

- Work on yourself and the presentation before your actual presentation. When David the shepherd boy singlehandedly killed the lion and the bear, little did he know that Goliath would soon be presented to him to fight and kill.
- Be clean and creative in your presentation. I suggest that students with poor handwriting ought to work on their handwriting as this may affect their grades.

What contributes to good Presentation?

- Good understanding of what is to be presented.
- Easy to follow, clean and creative presentation including legible handwriting.
- Orderliness.
- Good communication of presentation – pitched to the level of the audience and being current in affairs that relate to the presentation.

Where the Presentation is about the appearance of a person

- Good looks and smell.
- Clean outfit affordable to the person.
- An outfit that befits the occasion e.g. wearing the best

jeans for a bank or managerial job interview is most likely going to count against you.
- Good manners and orderliness.
- Healthy look.
- Confidence in God and in yourself.
- Good communication skills and being current in affairs that relate to the presentation.

Even where and when you have the same skill, qualification, knowledge or information with your competitor, oftentimes the person with the better presentation becomes the preferred candidate. Whilst your appearance/presentation will open the door, your manners will keep you in the presence of dignity and royalty.

Results of Good Presentation

You become the preferred/favoured person.

Results of Bad Presentation

You lose out in that competition.

Has my Presentation anything to do with my future?

Yes, presentation plays direct and indirect roles in your future. Example of direct role can be seen during examination or interview results and indirectly when people recommend you to higher authorities or for greater responsibility/position.

PRESENTATION

Exercise:

❖ How will you rate your school, college or work presentation at present?
❖ What are people saying about your physical presentation?
❖ What needs to change in your presentation?
❖ Identify what and who can help you achieve the required change and contact him/her immediately.
❖ What will be the indicators to confirm a better presentation from/by you?

Prayer Points:

Lord, thank You for making me so complex and beautiful.

Holy Spirit, please help me to enhance my God - given beauty and talents.

Lord, please teach me and help me to work on the following areas of my personal/professional presentation so that I might represent You well.

'Let's Reason Together ...Youths' A-Z

MY PERSONAL NOTES

QUEST

"Nothing ventured, nothing gained".

Before I was formed in my mother's belly, God knew me; and before I came forth out of the womb God sanctified me and ordained me a prophet unto the nations [Jeremiah 1:5 my paraphrase].

Questions for Consideration/ Discussion:
1. What is a quest?
2. Why have a quest?
3. Is God interested in my quest?
4. Is there a right or wrong quest?
5. How do I know which quest/vocation I should pursue?
6. My quest and my parents/community.
7. Quest influencers: what or who are these?

What is a Quest?

It is a mission, expedition, pursuit, assignment, task, calling, vocation, purpose, objective, aim, job, work, an occupation, a livelihood or line of business that you choose to follow.

Why have a Quest?

Every person God made is multi-skilled and multi-talented. Having a quest/vocation allows a person to harness his/her skills/talents into one or more occupations thereby bringing in an income or blessings to the person and community.

Is God interested in my Quest?

Certainly yes! Every person was created first to worship and have fellowship with God, to have dominion over all of God's creation and to fulfil a particular purpose in this world in whichever generation he/she finds him/herself.

God saw the need of each family or the community or world then He made each person to meet the various needs in our family/community/world.

QUEST

Is there is a right or wrong Quest?

There is no right or wrong mission/vocation/assignment but each person should seek the face of God, make use of every available career counselling service before deciding on which vocation path or route or calling to follow in life.

How Do I Know Which Quest I Should Pursue?

As you seek the face of the Lord in worship and prayers, He in His mercies may unveil His plans to you directly, through dreams/vision as in the life of Joseph [Genesis 37: 5-10], or through other people's comments about your inclinations. You need to also identify the various needs or challenges you can or would love to defeat and overcome. Your soft spot may indicate your calling/ quest/ mission or assignment. What is that thing (s) that you find easy to do or that you still enjoy doing even when you are very tired? It might be a pointer to what your calling is calling is e.g., if you enjoy playing with figures, perhaps you should consider a career in accountancy or statistics, if you enjoy travelling perhaps you should consider a mission or assignment that will encourage or include that. Equally what is that thing that upsets you most and you wish you could have an immediate solution to? It might be an indication of what you were created or destined to sort out. E.g. if you hate people around you falling ill/sick and each time you feel like doing everything to make a sick person better or healed then you ought to consider becoming a part of the health or intercessory or deliverance – healing ministry team. If you hate poverty and anyone around you suffering because of poverty then consider the financial careers. Your calling/ vocation might be hidden in your gifting or talents, take time to prayerfully find it out and use it. It might be hidden in your strength or weaknesses too so don't despise them. Peace comes with the right chosen vocation.

My Quest and my parents, Family/Community

Your chosen quest should directly or indirectly profit yourself i.e. make you feel fulfilled that you are doing what you were created/meant to do, for your parents, family and your community. Some parents might choose a career/ mission for their child without giving them any option – whilst it is good to support and harness a child's talent, the ultimate choice of your assignment/ mission/goal should be prayerfully left to that child except in instances where for example the child had been covenanted to God before or just after that child's birth e.g. *Samuel in 1Samuel:1:9-11, 20-28.*

QUEST

Quest influencers: what or who are these?

These are things or people who by your interaction with them influence your choice of pursuit, mission, assignment or objective positively or negatively.

Proposed income from a chosen career can also affect your choice.

GOOD INFLUENCES	INFLUENCES
God	Satan
Church	Cults, Bad Clubs
Good peers	Bad peers
Good Christian clubs	Drugs, cigarettes, alcohol or wine
Some parents, relatives and/or siblings	Also and unfortunately so, some parents, relatives and/or siblings

Don't go into a mission/vocation/pursuit/assignment where you cannot ask God to bless you or use you for His glory and mankind's blessings.

Exercise

- Identify your talents/skills.
- Is there any situation that makes you angry and you wish you could correct it?
- How can you enhance your talent/skill?
- Which profession/vocation are you likely to pursue and why?
- Identify any challenges that might want to distract you from fulfilling your quest in life and pray about this.

Prayer Point

Lord, please help me to identify my quest.

Lord, I commit my quest to You, take it and use it as You please.

Lord, please help so that I can make my quest relevant to my environment and family.

QUEST

MY PERSONAL NOTES

RESPECT

"Respect begets respect".

"Render therefore to all their dues: tribute to whom tribute is due; custom to whom custom; fear to whom fear; honour to whom honour" [Romans 13:7].

Questions for Consideration/Discussion
1. What is respect?
2. Who do we need to respect?
3. Is God interested in my respect?
4. Is there is a right or wrong way of showing respect?
5. Respecting myself.
6. Respecting my parents/community.
7. Respect and Pride – are they related?

What is Respect?

To respect another person or respect a thing means to hold in high opinion, high regards, admiration of others and high esteem.

Who do we need to Respect?

We need to respect God, the Creator and Sustainer of life, respect all others whom God has made as we come in contact with them. In respecting God, we will be careful to obey Him always when it is convenient and when it is not. We will be mindful how we treat other human beings and God's other creations and finally we will be watchful on how we treat ourselves.

Is God interested in my Respect?

Yes, He is completely interested as whatever respect or disrespect we have for Him, others and ourselves will have a significant bearing on our lives and relationship with Him. Anyone who has no respect for others and/or other creation of God is not likely to respect God.

RESPECT

Is there is a right or wrong way of showing Respect?

Different cultures have different ways of expressing respect. No single culture or nationality is inferior or superior to the other.

It is important that young people are able to identify how respect is expressed within their culture and utilise this and should they find themselves in another cultural setting, find out how to relate in this new setting and apply it where applicable. For instance within the Yoruba setting, the young people kneel or prostrate before adults whenever they come in contact with them especially in the morning or the first time you meet the adult in the day. Equally a pleura word is used for a single adult older than the young person when talking whereas in the UK for instance, it is not uncommon for a child or young adult to call the mother or another adult by his/her first name.

Respecting yourself

What you call yourself and/or the way you present yourself dictates the way people respect you or otherwise. Respecting yourself will be evident in how you treat yourself, what you say about yourself to others and yourself, and how you rate yourself publicly and privately.

Respecting your parents/community

Everything you do to others is a seed therefore be careful what you sow and how you sow your seed. Given the right conditions you will in this life reap whatever you sow into the lives of others including that of your parents and elders in your community. How respectful are you to your parents and elders in the community where you live, study or work? Respecting your parents is one of the many ways of honouring them. It does not matter if you are more educated, more gifted, more beautiful or handsome, more wealthy than your parents, you may be the one the Lord has blessed enough to look after or take care of them, you still must learn to and actually honour them as you respect them. Equally the way you show respect and love to your parents will influence how your friends treat them too.

Respect and pride – are they related?

They are not related. It is most difficult if not impossible to respect a person/thing and yet have pride towards that person or thing. Respect is a good Godly quality whilst

RESPECT

pride is one of the fruits of the flesh and it is sinful as well. God hates pride [Proverbs 16:18, 6:16-21]. Respect accepts others as God made them and honours them whereas pride demands that everyone else apart from themselves must bow down to them and worship them. Such a person will be full of pride and arrogance if care is not taken like Haman did to Mordecai in Esther 3:1-6.

Exercise:

◈ How easy is it for you to respect yourself and others?
◈ Who have you or are you disrespecting and why?
◈ How can you show respect to God and your parents?
◈ How can you show respect to your school, work authority?
◈ In which ways can you respect your Country?

Prayer Points:

Lord, help me to respect Your laws throughout my life.

Lord, please help me to show respect to my parents and those who have authority over me.

Lord, teach me and help me to treat with respect my body, talents and skills in Jesus' name.

RESPECT

SIN

"Sin is always secretive, seductive but never satisfies".

"Therefore to Him that knoweth to do good, and doeth it not, to Him it is accounted as sin" [James 4:17]

"Whatsoever is not of faith is sin" [Romans 14:23].

Questions For Consideration/ Discussion:
1. What is sin?
2. Why do we sin?
3. How do we sin?
4. With whom do we sin?
5. The results of a lifestyle of sinning.
6. How to get out of the lifestyle of sinning.
7. Sin shall no longer have dominion over me.

What is Sin?

Sin is anything that is done that displeases God. It could also mean or be an offence, felony, wrongdoing, misdeed, misbehaviour, misconduct, misdemeanour, evil doing, and law breaking. Any good that we know to do but refuse to do is sin. Sin always has a sweet and bitter part to it. It is done against God or and any of His creation e.g. stealing someone else's properties or telling lies about someone else, or backbiting or gossiping under the pretext of sharing prayer points, or pride/arrogance, fornication/adultery etc. (you may wish to identify more sins but use a few as the Holy Spirit will guide you in the discussion).

Why do we Sin?

We sin because we inherited the nature of Adam to sin. At other times, it is easier to sin than do things properly or it may seem easier to sin than to wait for God's promises to be fulfilled. At other times it may seem easier to sin than tell the truth about a situation and be deported if you are an illegal immigrant in a foreign land or easier to sin than tell the truth and be seen as a weakling, unhelpful or not part of the group etc., for example, living a lie.

SIN

How do we Sin?

The five senses of a man are the sense of sight, smell, taste, hearing and touch. Sin can be through any of these five senses or in our minds and in our thoughts. Devilish thoughts that are not quickly flushed away or erased will breed in any mind that is not constantly regenerated through the blood of Jesus Christ and the words of God as in the Bible; if care is not taken the person will begin to act on these wicked thoughts.

With whom do we Sin?

Sometimes we sin all by ourselves while at other times we get others innocently or knowingly involved. Eve not only disobeyed God by eating the forbidden fruit but she gave to Adam her husband *(Genesis 3)*. Achan stole the cursed items and hid them under the tent – an expensive disobedience and sin that caused Him his life and that of all the members of his family *[Joshua 7:1-26]*. Samson gave his parents some of the honey from the carcass of the dead lion without telling them *[Judges 13:1-4, 9-14, 14:1-9]*.

The results of a lifestyle of Sinning

The Bible says we should not be deceived, for whatsoever a man sows that he shall reap, sin inclusive. Every sin carries a reward, which is always negative. The rewards sometimes could come very quickly, instantaneously but some other time it could be delayed but sin's reward will surely come. The Bible says the wages of sin is death *(Romans 3:23)* and in *Romans 6:23* it says all have sinned and fallen short of the Glory of God. For anyone who continues a lifestyle of sinning can be guaranteed a payday for it. God will show mercy but hardly does any sin go unpunished. What more? To whom much is given, much is expected. Moses sinned and God did not spare Him *[Numbers 20:1-13]*. David's affair with Bathsheba resulted in a heavy punishment *[2 Samuel: 11-12]*. Adam and Eve sinned and God did not spare them *[Genesis 3]*.

Watch the thoughts you entertain, for out of your minds/thoughts, flows rivers of living waters *[Proverbs 23:7, Psalms 103:7-12]*.

How to get out of the lifestyle of Sinning

If you have not accepted the Lordship of Jesus Christ, you will need to do that first *[John 3:16-18]*. Secondly you will need to acknowledge the sin first that it exists in your life. Next you need to take time to seek the face of the Lord confessing that sin and asking God for the power to overcome this/that particular sin. You need to study and locate the appropriate/relevant passages in the Bible to read, learn, memorize and put to constant use especially when that particular sin tries to raise its ugly head against you again. 'Finally, brethren, whatsoever things are true, whatsoever things are honest, whatsoever things are just, whatsoever things are pure, whatsoever things are lovely, whatsoever things are of good report; if there be any virtue, and if there be any praise, think on these things' *[Philippians 4:8]*. You need to seek for Godly counsel and perhaps ask the Lord to choose for you a Godly Christian mentor in whom you should be able to confide, who will have time for you and who can monitor your progress against that sin, encouraging you, motivating you but not afraid to tell you that you are wrong and correct you in love. 'Confess your faults one to another, and pray one for another, that ye may be healed. The effectual fervent prayer of a righteous man availeth much' *[James 5:16]*. Your mentor should genuinely be interested in your progress especially in the area in which he/she is mentoring you. You might have to do away with things/family/friends/peers/places that encourage the atmosphere of sin around you lest they manage to keep you bound to that sin.

Sin shall no longer have dominion over You

*'Oh, be careful little eyes what you see,
Little mouth what you taste, eat or speak,
Oh be careful little hands what you do, touch or take,
Little ears what you hear, little legs where you go,
For the Father up above,
Is looking down in love…*

In line with the admonition of the lyrics of this popular Children's song, you will need to make your wish of getting out of any sin workable as you keep a close eye on your choices daily, constantly regenerating your mind with the word of God as in the Bible, praying and surrendering to God. The opportunities to fall into that sin will always come but with God's help through the Holy Spirit you will overcome.

SIN

What is your definition of sin, dear friend?
In a changing society like ours with changing ideologies,
Many have removed the word 'sin' form their dictionary,
To them it is one of those acceptable societal norms.

Sin to me, is not an illness, dear friend,
It is not a temptation nor problem,
It is not a mistake or normal,
It is that which is done of our choice.

Sin has a love and hatred relationship,
Men tend to love its false pleasures,
Hating themselves, or others, thereafter,
It is that which requires forgiveness.

Sin is dabbled into deliberately and consciously
It becomes addictive over time like a drug,
It never satisfies, no matter how much the amount,
It tends to be covered up with other sins.

Sin is incredibly destructive, dear friend;
It is the most expensive thing in this world,
It causes sickness and death of all kinds,
It finally sends the unrepentant sinner to hell's fire.

Sin causes a person untold loss of relationship,
It causes breaks in human relationships;
It causes communication breakdown with God;
It causes one to lose one's peace, respect and dignity.

Sin, expensive, as it was, had to be purchased,
It cost God His only begotten Son Jesus Christ;
It caused Jesus to leave Heaven and come to earth;
It caused Jesus to lay down His life on the cross.

Sin is sin in the sight of God, no matter what your excuse
It is an abomination in the sight of God,
It will be punished sooner or later, dear friend,
It is full of deadly poison and toxins.

Sin requires forgiveness first from God,
It does require admitting it and confessing it,
It requires our complete round about turn to good;
It requires conscious effort to forsake it through the Holy Spirit.

Sin's forgiveness first is from the Almighty God,
It needs forgiveness from those affected by it,
It needs the sinner forgiving Himself or herself;
It needs the blood of Jesus for complete cleansing.

SIN

Societal acceptance of that sin as a common norm,
Does not remove it from being sin in God's presence,
It does not remove its gravity or punishment,
Indeed the soul that sinneth will surely die.

Will you, dear friend, continue to toy with that sin?
Will you not remember that God is seeing it?
Will you stop refusing to admit this abomination?
Will you not today do away with that sin completely?
© O. Ola - Ojo 1992.

EXERCISE:

❖ What is your own definition of sin?
❖ Identify your secret sins and what has kept you repeating it/them.
❖ What is your sin costing you? e.g. money, lack of peace, abuse etc
❖ What can you do today to break the sin influence over you? Act on it.
❖ Identify and contact today a Godly same sex person who could mentor you as you try to eliminate that sin in your life.

** *Group coordinators should provide confidential same sex counselling and seek help if and where needed.*

PRAYER POINTS:

Lord, please forgive me, my family and community of all of our sins.

Lord, please help me to be aware of sin and avoid every sinful habit.

Holy Spirit, please abide in me and help me to overcome every bait of sinful habits in Jesus' name.

SIN

TRUTH

"The freedom I have is directly proportional to the truth I know and apply".

"And ye shall know the truth, and the truth shall make you free" [John 8:32].

Questions For Consideration/Discussion
1. What is truth?
2. Why do we need to know 'the truth'?
3. Truth and facts, which do, I prefer?
4. Truth and Freedom – how are they related?
5. Where can I find the truth for myself?
6. Is it possible to live in the truth always and how?

What is Truth?

A truth could be a piece of accurate information, evidence, a detailed statement, precise information, a reality that is of certainty, and/or authenticated information.

Difference between a truth and 'the Truth'

A truth refers to accurate information about something, person. With a truth, it means there are or might be some other truths on the same subject being discussed or considered. Jesus Christ when He was on earth said *'I am the way, the truth and life; no one gets to the Father except by me' [John 14:6].*

Jesus Christ was very clear, specific and direct not only about who He is but more so about His relationship with God and access to God by any human being. Indeed there is no other way to God except through Jesus Christ.

Truth and facts, which do i Prefer?

The facts will present all the evidence of a situation/condition as the experts in that field or subject know it. However the facts cannot save or deliver any person from any situation, only the truth can. For example a person is not feeling well and goes to the Doctor who after a series of tests comes up with the diagnosis, let us say fever. That is the fact but it cannot make that person feel better neither does it guarantee that the prescribed medication will cure that fever. The truth about fever is that Jesus Christ when He was alive rebuked fever from Peter's mother-in-law. *'And he arose out of the synagogue, and entered into Simon's house. And Simon's wife's mother was taken with a great fever; and they besought him for her. And he stood over her, and rebuked the fever; and it left her: and immediately she arose and ministered unto them' [Luke 4 38-39, Mark 1:30-31, Matthew 8:14-15].* The truth is to apply the words of God in the scriptures to the fever that person is experiencing and the symptoms must disappear with or without any medication depending on the level of that person's faith.

As a matter fact, you may not have the right course to pursue in the higher institution now but the truth is that God has a good plan and an expected end for each of His children. Being aware of that truth gives life and hope even in adverse times *[Jeremiah 29:11. Romans 8:28].*

Truth and Freedom – how are they related?

Freedom has many meanings including autonomy, liberty,

free-will, lack of restrictions and independence. Today, many people are either looking for the truth or for freedom. Truth about their origin, who they really are and what they are here on earth for. They are in search of the truth about some of the experiences of life they have or are going through when things don't make sense to them. Others are in search of freedom from all forms of sins and vile, they have tried all forms of 'modern day steps to recovery/therapy' that initially proved promising but with time they are back to where they started, if not worse! Others still are in search of deliverance/healing from all manners of diseases. Thank God for medical advancements and discoveries but there are still many diseases with no known cure in this 21st Century. What more? More complicated diseases are surfacing. Anyone who has ever experienced the limitation and pains of disease will more than likely try everything possible to get healing and be free again.

The crux of the matter is that there is no truth or freedom outside of Jesus Christ. He said *'I am the way, the truth and the life, no one comes to the Father except by Me'*. The Bible contains the truth and all it takes to be free and live free in the true sense. As you begin to search the Bible for your situation, the Lord will help you find the relevant scriptures and as you claim it and stand on God's promises, God will come through for you. For instance, there is the general believe that you have to work and strive hard to get to the top of

TRUTH

the ladder in your career/ field but the Bible says "it is not of him that runneth or of him that willeth but of God that showeth mercy."

Another scripture says, *'I returned, and saw under the sun, that the race is not to the swift, nor the battle to the strong, neither yet bread to the wise, nor yet riches to men of understanding, nor yet favour to men of skill; but time and chance happeneth to them all'* *[Ecclesiastes 9:11]* and another scripture says God wants us not to work round the clock, He actually wants His beloved some rest. Whatever experience/challenge you are facing, knowing the fact is good but knowing the truth as recorded in God' word is much better.

Why do we need to know 'The Truth'

God has meant for us to be successful, on top and not beneath in spite of our life challenges. Life could be though at times but getting to know Jesus Christ guarantees salvation, peace and victory. The truth as contained in the Bible will also help us to put everything in perspective and be assured of a breakthrough God's own way and in His own time. We would then not be fooled into seeking for help from other non-godly sources that usually delivers nothing and complicate matters.

Where can I find the Truth for myself?

You can find the truth for yourself in the Bible, in prayers and, as you fellowship with God with the help of the Holy Spirit; as you listen to the word of God being preached, taught or shared through different (one-on-one preaching, radio, television, print etc) media and from testimonies of others around you and around the world.

Is it possible to live in the Truth always and how?

Once you have given your life to Jesus Christ, it is possible but you must choose to find the truth about your situation in the Bible, believe it in the face of your situation and use it against the fact of your situation. God has not changed. For example, if you are having financial challenges, no matter how bad, one of the relevant scriptures to meditate upon is *Philippians 4:19* that says, 'But my God shall supply all of my needs according to His riches in Glory through Christ Jesus'. Note that the promise is:

My **(Your) God** – Jehovah Jireh. The word "My" is a personal pronoun and it is used by Apostle Paul to demonstrate a close and intimate relationship with God. It does not matter what others think of Him, the God that the apostle wrote about is the God that he knew personally and could predict accurately. Is He your God too or you are not really sure of the relationship you have with Him yet?

Shall supply – He is able and willing to supply

All of my needs – **all** not some, **my** – not someone else's, **needs** – not wants, but you will equally need to identify the needs and be specific about what exactly you want e.g. a brand new mountain bicycle to ride to school or a very good grade enough to get me into my chosen course and higher institution of learning etc.

According to His riches in Glory – in line with His heavenly wealth and not dependent on the earth's wealth or economy, not dependent on your income or savings, not dependent on your being or not being in gainful employment, not dependent on your worthiness or not, not dependent on whatever you have done or will do. God's riches and wealth cannot be exhausted by mankind's demands at any time or all the time.

Through Christ Jesus – that is the only name that allows us to draw our needs from the throne of grace. That is the only name that has been given above every other name in heaven, on earth and under the earth [Philippians 2: 9 –11]. That is the name to which all angels respond, elders bow down and worship, Satan trembles and flees. There is power, might, victory, blessings, healing, remarkable breakthrough in the name of Jesus Christ. God is in love with His children and like one preacher once said, He is looking for where and who to bless with His wealth. God's blessings are not man-made or tailored but full of compassion.

I'll love to share this write-up with you and pray that you are blessed as you read it.

BUT WHOSE REPORT WILL YOU BELIEVE?

The Doctors at last have come up with your diagnosis
They have come up with the prognosis of what to expect from now
The pains they say will never go away, the wounds won't heal
The condition they say may likely get worse as from now on
But whose report will you believe?

The bank statement is here again in the usual envelope
The account is not only red but very red with overdraft overdrawn
The creditors are at your tail with a threat of visit from the debt collector
The end of the tax year has come and your can't balance your books
But whose report will you believe?

TRUTH

The relationship is not over but it seems and feels well over
Communication between both of you is rather very sore
Commitment to make it work has lost its zeal and ability
Concern for each other's welfare is certainly lacking and obvious
But whose report will you believe?

The job is over when you have least expected
There is no other job in sight to keep you busy and thinking
There is your age and possibly your lack of much education
There is your family and other responsibilities to be concerned about
But whose report will you believe?

The situation you are in is very real dear friend
There is no running away from the obvious facts
There is no known human solution in sight
There is no man who could solve that problem
But whose report will you believe?

Time now to accept the facts as they lay before you
Time now to hand these facts to your Maker and Lord
Time now to seek for the truth about your situation in the Bible
Time now to turn your focus only on the truth as written in the Bible
Facts or truth the choice of your belief will determine the outcome

'Let's Reason Together ...Youths' A-Z

God's truths will any day override man's fact
For He speaks no careless word to anyone
His words are true, pure and sure to anyone who believes
He backs His word by name and Himself
Facts or truth, whose reports will you believe?
©Ola – Ojo 31.05.2003

Exercise:

- ◆ Identify any area of your life that needs freedom.
- ◆ Identify at least two Bible passages that address your need.
- ◆ Write them down, memorize them and meditate on them.
- ◆ Each time there is the urge for that need, recite those verses to yourself and God.
- ◆ Why do we focus on facts and not the truth of situations?

Prayer Points:

Lord, please help me to know You, the Truth.

Lord, please help me to know the truth about every situation that I am in or will be in as I go through life.

May I be set free by the knowledge of Your truth and may I also be an agent of sharing Your truth with all I come in contact with from now in Jesus' name.

'Let's Reason Together ...Youths' A-Z

MY PERSONAL NOTES

UNITY

"The united rule the divided".

"Behold, how good and how pleasant it is for brethren to dwell together in unity" [Psalms 133:1].

Question For Consideration/Discussion
1. What is unity?
2. Why do we need unity?
3. Causes of disunity?
4. How to maintain unity.
5. How to identify unity destroyers.
6. What is the 'divide and rule' concept?

What is Unity?

It means being in one accord, understanding one another, working together towards the same purpose, aim or goal, putting the group, family, society or community desired goal before personal gain or gratification. Unity that is being discussed here is Godly unity or unity to do something that will promote, permit good purpose and pursuit for mankind and our community.

Why do we need Unity?

A tree cannot make a forest. We all depend on one other and disunity will always bring set back, confusion, anger, lack of peace, distrust, inability to achieve one's goal or anything, working hard in circles but not achieving, avoidable and unnecessary wastage of time, resources and goals, avoidable aggravation. Unity permits progress, fulfils purpose and pursuit. United Nations rule divided nations. There is strength, power, progress and wealth in unity. There is exploitation and dissatisfaction in disunity.

UNITY

Causes of Disunity

- Putting self before the community or society or family.
- Sin, Satan or satanic interference.
- Distrust.
- Pride.
- Poor or wrong communication.
- External and/or ungodly influence who in any way benefits from disunity.
- Selfish thinking – me, I, my, mine, myself thinking.
- Immediate, local or limited gratification.

How To Maintain Unity
(not in any particular order)

- Fear of God and obedience to Him.
- Once you have a goal that is greater than yourself or resources, prayerfully look for those who have a similar or same goals that you can team up with.
- Define goals and strategies on how to achieve your goals.
- Having a common set goals/aims, purpose and always being aware of the goal.
- Delegate duties amongst yourselves.
- Let there be means of accountability within the group.
- Monitor goal's progress and maintain focus individually and collectively.

- ◈ Putting family or community or societal interest above self interest, i.e. think generationally - be future envisioned.
- ◈ Good communication which permits progress.
- ◈ Avoiding external influences who thrive on 'divide and rule'.
- ◈ Where there are people there is bound to be disagreements but we must learn to disagree to agree in such a way that our set goals for the community is not compromised but achieved at all cost.

What is the 'Divide and Rule' concept?

It is an ungodly wicked way of promoting disunity in a community, society or family or group such that there is distrust, fighting, killings, lack of purpose, a lot of wastage of time and resources, running in a circle like an hamster and not arriving or achieving goals/aims. Exploiters tend to use this tactic now and again. Their aim is to exploit each faction/fraction and indirectly control them, abuse and use the factions for their selfish, profitable goals. They cause all manner of distractions so that your goals are not achieved and you remain in perpetual modern day slavery always depending on them and so directly and indirectly controlled by them. They cunningly and tactically take your rich and empowering dialect, food, clothes etc. You must

UNITY

watch out for them, identify them and, resist them in the name of your Maker.

How to identify unity destroyers:

- ◈ Who or whatever undermines your goal in life.
- ◈ Who or whatever undermines your ability to achieve your goal.
- ◈ Time and resource wasters or delayers.
- ◈ Whoever causes miscommunication within your group or family or key players.
- ◈ Anyone that encourages you to discard all that is good and Godly in your culture e.g. as it relates to good home training, good and nourishing food and outfits.
- ◈ Attitude of pride or sinful behaviour.
- ◈ Anyone or anything that wants to rule your life, not giving you a chance to succeed or become who you were created to be.
- ◈ Anyone that thrives on disunity or pain or lack of progress in your life, family or community.
- ◈ Anyone that fuels disunity in your life, family or community.

EXERCISES

❖ Identify where there is unity or need for unity in your family or life.
❖ What are your goals in life?
❖ In what way do you intend to make your community, family or society better?
❖ Identify 'divide and rule' people or things around you.
❖ Ask God to help you to achieve your goals.

PRAYER POINTS:

Oh Lord, bring unity in my family, community and nation.

Lord, help me to learn to live and be in unity with those around me.

Lord, please make me a channel of unity and growth in my family, community and country in Jesus' name.

UNITY

VACATION

"Rest to my body is as important as good food to it".

"Jesus said to His disciples, Let us turn aside and rest awhile [Mark 6:31]"

"And the Lord rested on the seventh day [Genesis 2:2]

"Therefore everything there is a season and a time to every purpose on earth [Eccl.3:1]

Questions For Consideration/Discussion
1. What is it?
2. Who needs it?
3. Why do you need a vacation?
4. What makes a good vacation?
5. Is vacation only for the rich and wealthy?

What is It?

It is a planned time to be off one's routine or daily task or time taken off at the end of a project, business or work. For the student it is scheduled to be at the end of a school term, or school year/session. It is the time to rest and recuperate after studying and writing examinations or doing a project. For some it is the time to travel to their choice destination just for a holiday.

Who needs it?

Everybody needs the time to cool off, rest, travel if need be. God created the whole universe in six days and on the seventh day He rested. Jesus took the disciples aside so they could rest after a mission trip. God wants us to take a day at least every week to worship Him and rest.

Why do you need a Vacation?

We need times of vacations so that we can rest our physical bodies, take stock, worship God, appreciate other people, culture and other creations of God.

VACATION

What makes a good Vacation?

To me it means period of undisturbed rest, relaxing singly or in the company of friends and/or family, a time when you take time off your daily routines, a period of having undisrupted time with God and with one's self, it is a period of travelling to other parts of the world and appreciating other various cultures, etc. Sometimes you may just need to go somewhere quiet.

Is Vacation only for the rich and wealthy?

Absolutely no! Everyone should endeavour to have a vacation as often as possible. You do not need to travel far. You only need some space and time for yourself to rest, relax and be rejuvenated physically, emotionally and spiritually. You may consider a day trip to another part of your town or community or nearby town. Do something that you love and remember to give yourself a treat and some pampering.

EXERCISE:

❖ When last were you on a vacation?
❖ Share with the group what you did on that vacation?
❖ How did you feel after being on vacation?
❖ Will you want to go back to visit the place of your recent vacation? If yes why, if no why not?
❖ What steps have you taken or will you take to ensure you have a vacation periodically?

PRAYER POINTS:

Lord please provide for me and lead me to a good place for vacation.

As I go on my next vacation, please Lord make it the best time for me to have fellowship with You and with myself.

May all the blessings of a peaceful, restful vacation be mine in Jesus' name.

VACATION

WEALTH

"Health is wealth".

"I wish above all things that you prosper and be in health even as your soul prospers" [3 John 2].

Questions for Consideration/Discussion
1. What is wealth?
2. Why do we need to be wealthy?
3. How do people become wealthy?
4. Tips on how to become wealthy and maintain your wealth.
5. Health is Wealth.

What is it?

A wealthy person is one who has enough resources for his/her needs and extra to give to others in need directly or indirectly by employing them and paying their wages/salaries. For most people wealth is a gradual process. It is God's will for the child of God to prosper and be in good health and wealth. It is not a sin to be wealthy so long as you acquire your wealth in a Godly way and use it in a way to bless God and bring blessings to mankind.

Why do we need to be Wealthy?

1. For the believer i.e. Christian – God is the wealthiest and He created all from nothing. As His children we need to reflect and manage our heavenly Father's wealth whilst we are on earth. It reflects God's nature in us.
2. There will always be the poor around us in our community – it is the responsibility of the wealthy to look after these under-privileged ones.
3. We need to sponsor the Gospel message and other charity activities around the world.
4. We need to empower others get out of poverty, giving them opportunities by being an employer of labour.
5. To thank God.
6. Live a comfortable and affordable life with family.

7. Becoming a resource for/of money and wealth for many others.

How do people become wealthy?
(This is not in any particular order)

1. From inheritance – a good man leaves an inheritance for his grandchildren *[Proverbs 13:22]*
2. From hard work/labour – It is God's will for us to prosper in all our works.
3. Through property or money investments including, stocks, bonds, shares, etc.
4. From receiving God's divine intervention, connection, and marketing divine ideas e.g. Jacob in *Genesis 30:25-43*.
5. Through prospering as one uses one's gift to serve/minister to the needs of others e.g. Joseph in *Genesis 41:14-51, Daniel in Daniel 2:24-49*. A man's gift will make room for him *[Proverbs 18; 16, 28:27a, 19:17]*.
6. From receiving gifts from other people.
7. From their savings over the years.

Tips on how to become wealthy and maintain your Wealth (This is not in any particular order)

1. Acknowledge God as the real source of life and wealth.
2. In all your ways acknowledge God's help [Proverbs 3:5-6].
3. Pay your tithes on all income and gifts [Malachi 3: 10].
4. Give happily and generously to the work of the Ministry and people.
5. God is not a money doubler but He examines our motives for giving to His work or another man.
6. See all your giving as seeds, so sow generously with a defined purpose of your desired harvest in mind.
7. Be knowledgeable about what sort of investment channels you choose and be up to date with the chosen investment climate/result. Know the state of your flock - investments. Read good books on wealth, investments and autobiographies of wealthy people.
8. Be mindful of every divine idea. Such should be researched and pursued e.g. Jacob at the well.
9. The poor man's idea may die with him unless he/she finds a way for sponsors of the ideas. Beware of idea snatchers.
10. Learn not to eat all of your harvest, rather learn to operate on delayed gratification.
11. Be heavenly bound in spite of your wealth.
12. Learn to manage your wealth properly and not otherwise.

13. Be healthy and periodically give yourself a 'treat'
14. Have a grateful and humble heart always.
15. Be diligent and use your gifts to bless others [Proverbs 22:29].

Health is Wealth

What does this mean? Only a healthy person can be focussed on acquiring and managing wealth. Pay close and good attention to your health.

When should you begin?

Now! First you need to have a mindset of becoming wealthy. Most people build their wealth gradually i.e. over a period of time. Making becoming wealthy one of your goals in life is achievable. You need to be disciplined and have good self-control such that your outgoing is less than what comes in financially. This does not mean to be stingy but to be able to differentiate between needs and wants.

EXERCISE:

- ❖ Define what being wealthy means to you?
- ❖ What is in your hands e.g. skill, talent, or time that you can prayerfully work on and turn into wealth?
- ❖ What things do you see as obstacles to your becoming wealthy? e.g. bad habits or family curses etc.
- ❖ What things can you begin to do from now that will help you into getting into your wealthy place? e.g. working on your strengths or working towards eradicating your bad habits.
- ❖ Which books have you read or you are reading that will help you in your wealthy pursuit? Please share the lessons you have learnt with your group.

PRAYER POINTS:

God please empower me with the tools to use to become wealthy.

Father please grant me a sound health and wealth.

God, may You help me to be always be grateful to You and be a blessing to mankind with my wealth.

***Useful websites and books:*

- http://moneysense.natwest.com/natwest/info/about moneysense schools.
- http://moneysense.natwest.com/natwest/info/about_moneysense_adults.
- http://www.moneymadeclear.fsa.gov.uk/tools/compare_products.html
- freedomDebt.com – 800 978 0522
- **The 10 Ms Of Money** by Pastor Matthew Ashimolowo
- **Rich Dad, Poor Dad** by Robert T Kiyosaki
- **Poor Dad 2:** Cash Flow Quadrant - Rich Dad's Guide to Financial **Freedom** (Paperback) by Robert T Kiyosaki

'Let's Reason Together ...Youths' A-Z

Xenophobia

"All men are born equal"

"Be kindly affectioned one to another with brotherly love; in honour preferring one another" [Romans 12:10].

"Forbearing one another, and forgiving one another…" [Colossians. 3:13].

Questions for Consideration/ Discussion:
1. What is it?
2. Why are some xenophobic?
3. How to deal with a xenophobic?
4. If you are Xenophobic person.

What is it?

It means to be fanatical, racially prejudiced or intolerant. According to the Free Dictionary by Farlex, xenophobia could mean racism, sexism, ageism or religious intolerance with manifestations such as slavery, ethnic cleansing, religious persecution, genocide, hate crime race war etc. According to Encarta Dictionary: English UK, it means an intense fear or dislike of foreign people, their customs and culture or of foreign things.

What makes people to be Xenophobic?

Such people have intense dislike and fear of something which may be due to misconception or misinformation or lack of information about who or what thing they have xenophobia for. It could also be due to fear of their losing their land, home, national or tribal identity, faith, wealth to the foreigner or fearing them to do the abominable things e.g. sacrifice where it is being done today. It may be due to stereotyping of a person or thing,

In the days of the Bible the Israelites were oppressed and turned into slaves by 'a new king that arose that did not know Joseph' and who feared the Israelites might join forces with enemies to fight Egypt. He was very wrong but uncountable

Israelite babies and children were killed to weaken them *[Exodus 2:1-22]*.

Nathaniel stereotyped Jesus – *John 1:43-49*.

How to deal with a Xenophobic
(Not In Any Particular Order)

- Forgive their atrocities to you, your family or tribe or nation.
- Pray earnestly for them.
- Keep away from them if your life is not secured around such people.
- Avoid open confrontation but explore other means of communication with them if allowed or permitted.
- Report this attitude to the Police or law enforcement agent who can defend you.
- Do not ignore any threats however trivial – tell your family and trusted friends.
- Avoid being alone – let your family and friends know your movement – for your safety sake not for monitoring you.
- Be more vigilant so you are not attacked or assaulted unexpectedly.
- Avoid using the same route as the xenophobic person e.g same bus to school/work.

If you are the Xenophobic person

- Realize God made all in different colours, shapes, sizes, ages, tastes etc.
- Understand that there is enough space and wealth for all mankind.
- Appreciate the fact that each has the same life and breath and none is superior or inferior to the other.
- Realize that heaven is watching all your doings, none can be concealed from His eyes.
- One day you will face the consequences of your wicked action.
- You may not like other people's look or culture or belief BUT that does not give you any right or justification to kill or maim them in anyway.
- Ask God to teach you His love and be a person that will live and show His love.

XENOPHOBIA

EXERCISE:

- What makes people become xenophobic?
- ''All men and women are equal' - what does this mean to you?
- How can we be at peace with each other?
- How can you identify someone who is xenophobic?
- Pray as a group for understanding and God's true love in our community.

PRAYER POINTS:

Lord, please help me not to be xenophobic and remove any/every prejudice from me.

Lord please grant to me Your kind of Love.

Lord, please deliver me from all lions and xenophobic as I navigate in life in Jesus' name.

'Let's Reason Together ...Youths' A-Z

MY PERSONAL NOTES

YOKE

"It is better to bear the yoke of Christ than to wear the yoke of evil".

"And it shall come to pass in that day, that his burden shall be taken away from off thy shoulders, and his yoke from off thy neck, and the yoke shall be destroyed because of the anointing" [Isaiah 10:27].

"For my yoke is easy, and my burden is light [Matthew 11:30]

Questions for Consideration/Discussion
1. What is a yoke?
2. How do we get into a yoke?
3. Where and why do we use yokes?
4. What does unequal yoking means?
5. Can a Christian be under yoke?
6. How to destroy ungodly yokes.

What is a Yoke?

It may be a burden, bondage or form of oppression or repression.

How do we get into a Yoke?

Sometimes unknowingly and sometimes knowingly, sometimes we are born into the situation that oppresses us and prevents us from getting or being the best in life. E.g. people born with a congenital disease or malformations or people who are born into families with some peculiar negative history which might be as a result of a curse or covenant their forefathers might have made, e.g. the Gibeonites in *Joshua 9:3-21*.

Sometimes people enter seemingly initially appearing harmless relationships/friendships or they may eat or drink or take presents only to find that they have been yoked e.g. those who join cults etc.

Where and why do we use Yokes?

Yokes are generally used as a means of oppression or exploitation. It is oppressing the weak, vulnerable, inexperienced, gullible, lazy and those who are after getting rich or powerful quickly and cheaply.

What does unequal Yoke means?

It is being in agreement or in sole tie relationship with any ungodly person or thing or cult.

Can a Christian be under a Yoke?
Yes.

How to destroy ungodly Yokes
(Not In Any Particular Order)

- Give your life to Jesus Christ and have a meaningful relationship with Him,
- Ask God to open your spiritual eyes and ears to your personal or family circumstances.
- Ask God for the spirit of discernment.
- Ask God for divine wisdom on how to get out of the yoke without any negative repercussion.
- Identify one or two Godly people and seek for their counsel on the issue/s.

- Avoid anyone or anything that will not want you to be free from the yoke.
- Search, write out on a card, memorize and meditate on at least three scriptures to use against the enemy.
- Declare to yourself as many times as it is possible your new liberty in Christ Jesus. For if the Son shall set you free, you shall be free indeed.

Exercise:

- To who or what have you been yoked?
- Give examples of unequal yoking
- Identify any ungodly yoke that you bear.
- Ask God in prayers for the wisdom to get rid of all ungodly yokes.
- How can you identify potential yokes?
- What can you do to avoid ungodly yokes?

Prayer Points:

God please forgive me for getting unequally yoked.

Father please order my steps so that I may avoid all seen and unseen yokes.

God please help me not to be unequally yoked.

'Let's Reason Together ...Youths' A-Z

ZEST

"I am who I am by the Grace of God".

"I can do all things through Christ who strengthens me"
[Philippians 4:13].

Questions for Consideration/Discussion
1. What is it?
2. How do I know my zest?
3. Is my zest linked with my destiny in life?
4. How can I maximise my zest?

What is It?

Zest could mean something that you have passion for, devoted to, eager or keen to achieve, enthusiastic for, delight in, have pleasure for, or interested in.

How do I know my Zest?

You may need to take some time to examine your life or ask your trusted family members or friends to help you. It is likely to be that thing that you still enjoy to do even when you are tired, or never tired of doing or that thing that brings joy, excitement to you in spite of your circumstances. For example, if I have a free hour, I will joyfully crawl to my computer and do some writing. For you it could be drawing, working on hard sums, designing, cooking, painting, running, having a conversation with others etc.

Is my Zest linked with my destiny in life?

Most likely yes – directly or indirectly! You are likely to spend more time on what excites you, what you enjoy doing or what gives you pleasure than otherwise. If prayerfully and carefully harnessed this might point you in the direction of your life's destiny. E.g. those who from their youth are passionate about defending others or speaking on behalf of others often end up as lawyers or human right activists or politicians whereas those who are passionate about health issues end up in one arm of medical care.

Those who are keen on fine details often end up as scientists, accountants, designers or architects.

How can i maximise my Zest?
(Not In Any Particular Order)

- Ask God to show you your purpose in this life.
- Identify one or two of your zest.
- Prayerfully consider what you would like to become say in five years from now.
- Identify what you would need to do to achieve your goal.
- Identify courses or people who can be of help for you to achieve your goal.
- Pursue courses that can enhance your zest.
- Be around those in whose company you can learn more and use your zest.
- Avoid all zest killers e.g. bad habits, wrong company, wrong crowd or confessions.
- Prayerfully work with God on your zest and don't forget to give Him the praises for your achievements however small.

Exercise:

- Identify your zest.
- Identify three people or some courses that can enhance your zest.
- In about five years time where do you intend to be with your zest?
- What steps have you taken or will you take to enhance your zest.
- Read at least one autobiography of someone who has excelled in your chosen zest and share the lessons you have learnt from that person with the group or your friends.
- Identify potential killers of your zest and what you need to do to avoid them.

Prayer Points:

God thank You for giving me the liking and ability for my zest.

Father please send me godly friends and associates and helpers of destiny and empower me in my zest.

God please help me to glorify You and be a blessing to mankind with my zest.

MY PERSONAL NOTES

SUMMARY

A: **Attitude**
"My attitude will determine my altitude in life".

B: **Bible**
"The Bible is my atlas for a successful life".

C: **Choices**
"My choice will either make me or break me".

D: **Dream**
"My future is concealed in my dreams therefore I will dream big".
"God's revelation needs no second opinion"
"Godly dreams hardly die unfulfilled".

E: **Endurance**
"All of life's experience are meant to shape and sharpen us unto God's own person'
"We shall reap in due season if we faint not".

F: **Forgiveness**
"It is in forgiving others that we receive our forgiveness from God."

G: **Giving**
"He/she who cannot receive should not give".
"You can only give from that which has been given to you"

H: **Humility**
"My promotion lies in my humility and hard work".

I: **Integrity**
"I must let my yes be yes and nay be nay".

J: **Justice**
"*Righteousness exalts a nation/ a people*".

K: **Knowledge**
"*I who know my God shall be strong and do exploits*".

L: **Love**
"*Love God and love others as yourself*".

M: **Miracles**
"*Miracles are still every time occurrence with God*".

N: **Networking**
"*Evil association corrupts good manners*".

O: **Oath**
"*Be a man or woman of your words*".

P: **Presentation**
"*People see me before they hear me or get to know me*"

Q: **Quest**
"*Nothing ventured, nothing gained*".

R: **Respect**
"*Respect begets respect*".

S: **Sin**
"*Sin is always secretive and seductive and never satisfies*".

T: **Truth**
"*The freedom I have is directly proportional to the truth I Know*".

U: **Unity**
"*The united rule the divided*".

V: **Vacation**
"*Rest to my body is as important as good food to it*".

W: **Wealth**
"Health is wealth".

X: **Xenophobic**
"All men are born equal".

Y: **Yoke**
"It is better to bear the yoke of Christ than to wear the yoke of evil".

Z: **Zest**
"I am who I am by the grace of God".

OPPORTUNITY TO BECOME A CHRISTIAN

Dear Father in heaven,

Thank you for the privilege of reading this book. Indeed I have sinned and come short of Your glory. I am grateful to You for sending Jesus Christ into this world to come to die on the cross of Calvary for me. I believe in my heart that Jesus Christ paid for my sins, past, present and future. I believe Jesus Christ was buried and on the third day He rose from the dead. I believe that Jesus Christ will come back again. I confess with my mouth and I accept Him now to be my Lord.

Master, Saviour, Brother, and Friend, I ask in Your mercy for the infilling of the Holy Spirit so that with His help, I can live a victorious life becoming all that You have ordained me to be in Jesus' name. I pray with thanksgiving. Amen.

If after reading this book you said the above prayer and became born-again, Congratulations! You are Born Again is a booklet for those who have done so through reading this book. It is a free booklet that we would like you to have. In it, the frequently asked questions are answered and this will get you on the way to growing in your newfound faith in God. You can download this free booklet from our website: www.protokospublishers.com

You may also contact any of the organisations listed at the end of the book.

I look forward to hearing from you soon.
O. Ola−Ojo (2010)

Other Books By The Author:

Provocation, Prayer and Praise
(December 2004 & 2009)

Complimentary to The Christian and Infertility this book focuses on the story of an infertile woman in the Bible, her provocations, prayer and praise. Whatever makes you incomplete, unfulfilled, less than whom God made you to be, whatever issue of life that the enemy uses to provoke you calls for prayer.

Key features include:
- Some known medical reasons for infertility in the women.
- Why Hannah went to the house of God in spite of her barrenness.
- Is it true that the husband is much more than 10 sons to the infertile woman?
- When, where and how to address the source/cause of your provocation.
- God's part and your part in that promise.
- God is able to met that humanly impossible need of yours.
- A time to celebrate and praise God.

Book Details:
Paperback: 128 pages
Language English
ISBN-13: 978-0-9557898-3-0

A Reader from London, 7 Jan 2006 on Amazon.co.uk
An excellent easy to read and understand book. The principles shared in this book though primarily are for those trying for a baby could as well be applied to any area of hurt and un-fulfilment.

:www.protokospublishers.com

OTHER BOOKS

The Christian and Infertility
(December 2004 & 2009)

The Christian and Infertility addresses one of the often neglected needs of Christian couples. It gives an insight into infertility from the biblical and medical perspectives. It is written not only for potential fruitful couples but for pastors, family and friends of these couples. It is written that the Body of Christ might be fully equipped to know and support couples who are facing the challenge of infertility at present.

Key features include:
- Childleness in the Bible and lessons to learn;
- Some possible physical, medical and environmental causes of infertility;
- Some known spiritual causes of infertility;
- The man and low sperm count;
- Some of the available treatment optons in the UK;
- Choice of fertility treatment;
- Should a christian professional be involved in fertility treatment?

Book Details:
Paperback: 146 pages
Language English
ISBN-13: 978-0-9557898-2-3

A reviewer from Glen Burnie, USA, 29 Oct 2007 on Amazon.co.uk'
The book is a great eye-opener for all. It sheds light on infertility from the medical and spiritual angle. This gives the reader a balance because i believe every human being is made up of both physical and spiritual part. To get a balance in life, the two parts must be well fed. One must not concentrate on the spiritual and neglect the physical part. The book also reminds us that God has a way of sorting us out.... The book is quite inspiring. I will recommend this book to everybody trusting God for any form of blessing from God to go get one and apply it to his or her situation. It will definitely bless you and yours'.

 :www.protokospublishers.com

OTHER BOOKS

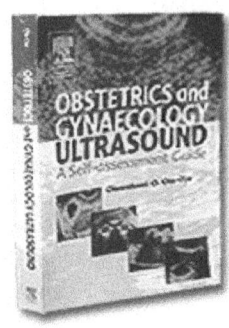

Obstetrics and Gynaecology Ultrasound -
A Self-Assessment Guide
June 2005 Churchill Elsevier Publishers, UK.

This self-assessment guide is a structured questions and answer book that develops the reader's understanding capability using a simple method in treating related topics. Clinical indications are presented with their corresponding ultrasound findings using appropriate illustrations. A case study approach is followed; presenting the clinical and ethical dilemmas that might arise whilst encouraging students to think. The aim is to reinforce theoretical knowledge within a clinical environment.

Key features:
- Over 600 high-resolution ultrasound images
- Cover a wide spectrum of ultrasound curriculum.
- Includes a detailed study of fertility.
- Aids quick understanding of subject matter.
- 468 pages.

ISBN-10: 0443064628
ISBN-13: 978-0443064623
Book Dimensions: 24 x 16.8 x 2.6 cm

"...This excellent new book is a study guide... This is an attractive paperback that should be essential reading for trainee obstetric and gynaecological sonographers, whether they are radiographers or radiology or obstetric trainees. It will be of particular value to those preparing for the RCOG/RCR Diploma in Advanced Obstetric Ultrasound and to specialist registrars in obstetrics and gynaecology undertaking special skills modules in fetal medicine, gynaecological ultrasound and infertility..."

The Obstetrician & Gynaecologist, www.rcog.org.uk/togonline
Book reviews 2006

Reviewer **Ann Harper MD FRCPI FRCOG.**
Consultant Obstetrician and Gynaecologist
Royal Jubilee Maternity Service, Belfast., UK

 :www.protokospublishers.com

OTHER BOOKS

GOOD MUMS, BAD MUMS
(June 2005 & 2009)

This is in two parts, the main chapter that can be used for personal or group study, and an accompanying exercise section. The privileged position of a mother is in her being a co-creator with God and bringing forth life (lives). This book compliments one of God's previous revelations to me as contained in the book titled Good Dads, Bad Dads'. While the father could be likened to the pilot of the family plane, the mother can be likened to the force behind the plane – positive or negative. Good mothers are not only co-creators with God, they also do nurture as well as nourish their children physically, emotionally and spiritually.

Keys Features:
- Were all the mothers in the Bible god mothers?
- Lessons from the strengths and weakness of seven mothers.
- Be encouraged - you are not alone in the assignment of motherhood.
- Be motivated in the areas of your strengths.
- Learn ways of supporting your husband and children.

Book Details:
Paperback: 162 pages
Language English
ISBN-13: 978-0-9557898-1-6
Book Dimensions: 21.4 x 14 x 1.4 cm

I appreciate the author's method of writing. It is always exciting holding her book to read. Personally, 'Good Mums, Bad Mums' has been a blessing to me in no small measure. The book is rich, it is loaded with physical and spiritual uplifting subjects. To all existing and potential mothers, this book is a MUST read. At the end of every chapter there is an exercise to do that will help in re-examining your life spiritually and in other ways. I encourage all women to get and use this book as a guide in raising their children. You will be glad you did.

Pastor Mrs T Adegoke
Freedom Arena
London, UK

 :www.protokospublishers.com

OTHER BOOKS

To the Bride with Love
(2007 & 2009)

Every wise woman preparing to get married knows she will need sound advice, practical tips and solid, heartfelt prayers, of those who have travelled on the road she is about to journey on. In this book, 10 women of different age groups, from different backgrounds and cultures who wedded under various circumstances, individually share their experience with the bride in an intimate, very candid and unforgettable way.

Book details:
Paperback: 108 pages
Language English
ISBN-13: 978-0-9557898-4-7
Book Dimensions: 22.4 x 15 x 1 cm

To the Bride with Love is the perfect bride's evergreen companion. The content is suitable, relevant and applicable even decades after the wedding day.

To the Bride with Love is an ideal wedding gift on its own. It can also accompany any other gift (big or small) that you have for the bride but take this hint... the bride will keep thanking you for the book years and years after.

'One of the best', 19 Jul 2008 on Amazon.com
Sade Olaoye "clare4good" (United Kingdom)
This book has really helped my marriage from the onset as I got it as a wedding gift, God bless the giver. It's a must read fro relationship improvement and God's guidance. I recommend people to get for oneself and also as a great blessing for someone else in love. "To the Bride with Love"

Review by Oyinlola Odunlami CEO.
Shallom Bookshop, London UK

The writing style of Oluwakemi is unique, peculiar and distinct to herself. I recommend To the Bride with Love to wives, wives to be, mothers, mentors, youth leaders and workers. Why? The clarity, the focus and the intent of this book is so empowering, encouraging and enlightening

OTHER BOOKS

that it will definitely mould or re mould a life to achieve its purpose. The truth is, there are very few books that have depth as well as help you to achieve your goals and arrive at your destination. Many books tend to excite you but have no depth; you read and you forget; they do not really change you but this book, To the Bride with Love will definitely leave a word in your spirit and move you to your next level!

I believe that this is also a book that pastors will find useful as a manual for marriage counselling, because many books on marriage focus mostly on what you as an individual can gain, your own personal satisfaction while little is said about the sacrifices involved and their importance. As my pastor usually says, it is important to learn from those who have gone ahead, understand why some were successful and others weren't, so that we won't fall where they fell, rather, we would gain more speed, achieve our goals and thereby glorify Christ.

So, I invite you not only to get a copy of this life-changing manual for yourself, but also to put it into as many hands as you can afford to, for then the world will definitely benefit and your life will be a blessing to many.

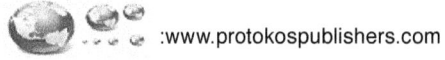
:www.protokospublishers.com

OTHER BOOKS

Refuge Under His Wings

"an exhaustive analysis of the Book of Ruth in the Bible. The author combines her deep Christian conviction and excellent knowledge of the Holy Scriptures to produce a must read for every Christian, married or single. The book is interspaced with beautifully written prayers, which enables the reader to pause, pray and meditate on the revelations received... The book is also loaded with poetry like 'Thy will be done oh Lord' for those who may be facing an uncertain future or on a cross road of decisions."

Dr E B Ekpo MD, FRCP
Queen Elizabeth Hospital, Christian Fellowship,
Woolwich, London. UK

"...[a] ...spiritually sound book... a fine work of thoughtful reading and study... I therefore recommend it to every Christian, married or single....
Pat Roach Senior Pastor
New Covenant Church.
Wandsworth Branch, London. UK.

Book details:
Paperback: 100 pages
Language English
ISBN-10: 095578980X
ISBN-13: 978-0955789809

This book feeds the soul. Most of all I loved the poetry. It gives you time to savour the thoughts as reader. There is a good mix of poetry and prose.To look at the story of Ruth in depth gave good spiritual food. You can pause and take it in at your own pace.The meditation on Psalm 121 was good also. There's nothing like reading a Psalm slowly and meditating on its contents. The author's own reflections allow you to see the book through someone else's eyes. A good read.

Book Review: by Gaby Richards, London, UK.

 :www.protokospublishers.com

OTHER BOOKS

GRACE OR WORKS

This book makes you examine a lot of issues in your life, family relationships in particular, that you may have taken for granted or totally ignored. As conveyed right from the rhetorical question posed in the title, Grace or Works, the author stirs you towards asking yourself pertinent questions, thinking through for answers and even getting solutions for unresolved problems.

Have you heard of prodigal wives, husbands, mothers or prodigal fathers? This book identifies and defines them clearly. For anyone experiencing a crises in their relationship with such prodigal family members, this book, which is based on the parable of the "Prodigal son" in Luke 15:11-32 is a one-stop resource material to meet your counselling needs. And just in case you happen to be the prodigal who has caused your relatives much sorrow, there is hope for you in this book.

Interspersed with prayers for you by the author and specific prayers that you can say for yourself, as well as poems to comfort and inspire you, Grace or Works not only asks you questions, it helps you make and maintain the right choices.

Book details:
Paperback: 122 pages
Language English
ISBN-13: 978-0-9557898-5-4

:www.protokospublishers.com

OTHER BOOKS

THERE IS A REWARD FOR PARENTING

Man may claim that the conception of a particular child was accidental, but in God's eyes every child is in His plan and has a purpose and mission to fulfil here on earth. As a parent, teacher, church or community leader, how are you treating the children in your care?

God does not sleep nor slumber; are you sure you are doing what He expects of you as a parent or children's Sunday school teacher? What kind of reward do you expect from Him?

There is a Reward for Parenting provides a lot of answers and food for thought, using scriptural principles to show you how to ensure a good reward from God in the unique assignment of parenting and child care.

As characteristic of Oluwakemi Ola-Ojo's previous books, there is a free gift of her poems at the end of this book also, to add value to the content of the main text – making it two books for the price of one!

Book details:
Paperback: 88 pages
Language English
ISBN 978-0-9557898-6-1

 :www.protokospublishers.com

COMING OUT SOON

- LET'S REASON TOGETHER - YOUTH'S A-Z. (BOOK 2)
- GOOD DADS, BAD DADS.
- INSPIRATIONS FOR THE MAN OF VALOUR.
- INSPIRATIONS FOR THE MAN OF COURAGE.

USEFUL ADDRESSES & WEBSITES

Care for the Family
PO Box 488
Cardiff
CF15 7YY
Tel: (029) 2081 0800
Fax: (029) 2081 4089
Email: mail@cff.org.uk
Website: www.care-for-the-family.org.uk OR www.cff.org.uk
Care for the Family aims to promote strong family life and to help those hurting because of family breakdown. Their heart is to come alongside people in the good times and in the tough times – bringing hope, compassion and some practical, down-to-earth help and encouragement.

Children Evangelism Ministry Inc
P.O. Box 4480
Ilorin, Kwara State,
Nigeria.
Tel: +234 31 222199
E-mail: cem@ilorin.skannet.com OR cem562000@yahoo.com
Children Evangelism Ministry Inc is a ministry that reaches out with the Gospel to children before and after birth. The ministry teaches and equips parents, teachers and coordinators of Sunday Schools and Children's Clubs. They also have and hold Children's Clubs, conferences and training seminars.

Focus on the Family
Tel: 1-800 - 232 6459
Website: www.family.org
Focus on the Family cooperates with the Holy Spirit in disseminating the Gospel of Jesus Christ to as many people as possible, and, specifically, to accomplish that objective by helping to preserve traditional values and the institution of the family.

'Let's Reason Together ...Youths' A-Z

Open Gate
2 Union Road
Croydon
CR0 2XU.
Tel: 0208 665 5533
Fax: 0208 684 7233
e-mail: opengate@yahoo.co.uk
           alteschool@yahoo.co.uk
Open Gate Provides a preventative and supplementary educational facility for youths at risk of permanent exclusion. We aim at empowering and connecting the youths for the future. We provide support for the family and the community.

Protokos Publishers
P.O. Box 48424
London
SE15 2YL
www.protokospublishers.com
Protokos Publishers provides various resources for the family. We publish many life's enlightening, informative and motivational must read books. With each of our books, you are guaranteed a 24/7 counsellor by your side on the subject.

The Shepherd's Ministries
5 Brookehowse Road
Bellingham
London SE6 3TJ, UK
Tel/Fax: +44 208 698 7222
Email: info@theshepherdsministries.org
Website: www.theshepherdsministries.org
The Shepherd's Ministries helps to bring children into an experience of worshipping God in truth and in spirit; give children a world-view based on God's word and mission and helps children to exercise their gifts in local and global missions.

'Let's Reason Together ...Youths' A-Z

Teenagers' Outreach Ministries (TOM) Inc.
Plot 85
Ladi Kwali Ext. Layout,
P.O.Box 16
Kwali, Abuja.
Nigeria.
Tel- 02082933730
Fax-02082933731
Nigeria - 08037044195
 - 07081860407
Email- tominthq@yahoo.co.uk
Website -www.tominternational .org
The Teenagers' Outreach Ministries (TOM) Inc. has a vision of leading today's teenager to Christ. This forms the foundation on which we mould their character in line with the word of God, thereby equipping them to fulfil their God ordained roles in life.

Total Woman Ministries
The Total Woman Ministries,
3 Herringham Road
Thames Wharf Barrier,
Charlton,
London
SE7 8NJ.
Tel: 020 8293 3730
Fax: 020 8293 3731
Email: admin@totalwomanministries.org
Website:www.totalwomanministries.org
Total Woman Ministries by God's grace has the sole vision of reaching out to women of all categories (married, single, separated, divorced, young, middle-aged or elderly).

United Christian Broadcasting UCB
P.O. Box 255, Stoke on Trent,
ST4 8YY, England
Among other forms of spreading the Gospel, UCB prints The Word For Today – a free daily devotional reading available for residents in the UK and Republic of Ireland

Dear Reader,

Thank you for your time and resources committed to supporting this writing ministry. Please help to tell others about how much the Lord has blessed you reading this book.

You will certainly be blessed by the other books written by Oluwakemi, so why not visit www.protokospublishers.com and place an order today.

It will equally be appreciated if you can help to write a few sentences review of the book on www.amazon.com and / or on www.protokospublishers.com.

Please note that all our books are easily available on our website and other good bookshops.

God bless you as you do.
Management
Protokos Publishers.

www.ingramcontent.com/pod-product-compliance
Ingram Content Group UK Ltd.
Pitfield, Milton Keynes, MK11 3LW, UK
UKHW020719050526
12271UKWH00018B/221